How to Make Beautiful Blooms & Turn Paper to Petals with Paper Flower Making

By Cindy Dreyer

© **Copyright 2017 by Cindy Dreyer - All rights reserved.**

This document is geared towards providing exact and reliable information in regards to the topic and issue covered. The publication is sold with the idea that the publisher is not required to render accounting, officially permitted, or otherwise, qualified services. If advice is necessary, legal or professional, a practiced individual in the profession should be ordered.

- From a Declaration of Principles which was accepted and approved equally by a Committee of the American Bar Association and a Committee of Publishers and Associations.

In no way is it legal to reproduce, duplicate, or transmit any part of this document in either electronic means or in printed format. Recording of this publication is strictly prohibited and any storage of this document is not allowed unless with written permission from the publisher. All rights reserved.

The information provided herein is stated to be truthful and consistent, in that any liability, in terms of inattention or otherwise, by any usage or abuse of any policies, processes, or directions contained within is the solitary and utter responsibility of the recipient reader. Under no circumstances will any legal responsibility or blame be held against the publisher for any reparation, damages, or monetary loss due to the information herein, either directly or indirectly.

Respective authors own all copyrights not held by the publisher.

The information herein is offered for informational purposes solely, and is universal as so. The presentation of the information is without contract or any type of guarantee assurance.

The trademarks that are used are without any consent, and the publication of the trademark is without permission or backing by the trademark owner. All trademarks and brands within this book are for clarifying purposes only and are the owned by the owners themselves, not affiliated with this document.

Table of Contents

Introduction 1

Chapter 1 – How did it All Begin? 3

   A Short History of Paper Flowers 3

   Reasons to Prefer Paper Flowers over Fresh Flowers 7

Chapter 2 – Equipment and Materials You Need for your Paper Flower Making Kit 10

   Basic Materials and Equipment 10

   Additional Materials and Equipment 11

   Basic Parts of a Paper Flower 13

Chapter 3 - Origami and Kirigami Paper Flowers 15

   Origami Paper Flowers 15

      Traditional Origami Flower 16

      2-Piece Traditional Origami Flower 22

      Origami Rosettes 27

      Cherry Blossom 31

      Five Petal Flower 35

      Paper Fan Flowers 39

      Tulip 43

      Lily 48

      Kusudama (Modular Origami) 54

   Kirigami Paper Flowers 58

Carnation	59
8-Petal Kirigami Flower	61

Chapter 4 – Long Strip Paper Flowers ... 63

3D Paper Flowers	63
Daisy	64
Calendula	67
Lavender	71
Simple Rose	74
Method 1:	74
Method 2	76
Peony	79
Narcissus or Daffodil	84
Marigold	91
Sunflower	94
Delphiniums	97

Chapter 5 – Integrated Paper Flowers ... 99

Carnation	100
Hibiscus	102
Calla Lily	105
Roses	108
Anthurium	112
Tulip	115
Anemone	117
Iris Flower	120

Poppy Flower 123
Birds of Paradise 127
Chapter 6 – Cluster Flowers.. 133
Lily in the Valley 134
Wisteria 137
Apricot Flowers...141
Baby's breath.. 145
Delphiniums..148
Bells of Ireland 152
Gladiolus 155
Chapter 7: Flower Buds 161
Carnation, Hibiscus and Poppy Buds................ 162
Rose Buds.. 165
Tulip 168
Calla Lily Buds 170
Iris Flower and Narcissus Bud 171
Daisy, Sunflower and Calendula Bud.................175
Calendula bud 177
Anemone 179
Poppy Flower Buds 181
Half-bloom Bud.. 183
Anthurium Bud 184
Peony Bud 185
Chapter 8: Simple Projects Using Paper Flowers.. 188

- Scented Flower Vase 188
- Flower Pomanders 191
- Flower-Bordered Picture Frame 194
- Paper Flower Crowns 198
  - Easy Daisy Crown 201
  - Easy Baby's Breath Wreath or Crown 203
- Paper Flower Designed Jars 205
- 2D - 3D Mural 207
- Fake Terrariums 208
- Conclusion 210

Introduction

Thank you for purchasing this book, "Paper Flowers: How to Make Beautiful Blooms & Turn Paper to Petals with Paper Flower Making."

Flowers, regardless of their shape, size, variety, number and color, can add beauty and elegance to almost anything. Most houses, parties, weddings, or events use flowers to decorate the venue or to add lovely colors to the place.

Using fresh flowers is always the best option. We have to admit that fresh flowers stimulate our senses. It magically adds a relaxing and elegant ambiance. However, using a lot of them may not be practical. Most of them can only last a month, but even then, they would not remain as beautiful and fresh.

One option to maintain the beauty or elegance of the room or event is to use artificial flowers. There are many types of artificial flowers. They can be made out of silk fabric, plastic and paper. Among these substitutes, paper flowers are deemed to be the easiest to make. You do not need any machinery or expensive materials to create them. Most of the materials and equipment you need can be found in your home.

Some of them can be bought in a nearby craft store and are also sold cheaply.

Using paper to make flowers allows you almost boundless creativity. And, that is what this book will help you realize. It will help you spark some of that often overlooked imagination you've kept hidden. It will teach you steps and strategies on how to make lovely, beautiful and elegant paper replicas of many different types of flowers.

With this book, you would now be able to decorate your house, or any of party venues with any flower you might want to use. You do not have to worry about ordering, harvesting or keeping it fresh. This book will also help you save on your budget for those beautiful, rare and/or out-of-season flowers.

I hope you will learn and enjoy this craft through my book.

Chapter 1 – How did it All Begin?

A Short History of Paper Flowers

The art of making artificial flowers has existed for more than five thousand years. The older versions of artificial flowers were made with fabrics or dyed fibers of plants and animals.

The second material that was used to make artificial flowers was paper. Though many history books claim that it was the Europeans, who started making paper flowers, there are evidence that opposes this fact.

During 50AD, a Chinese inventor named Cai Lun discovered paper by recycling the fibers of silk. Realizing that the new sheets can also be used for writing messages, he suggested to the emperor of the Han Dynasty that they should substitute silk with paper. The messages written in the paper were easier to hide and destroy. It was also faster to make and cheaper. He also proposed that using paper as a substitute would also increase the bulk of silk that China could export to Europe and the rest of Asia.

Soon, the uses of paper were not limited to simply writing messages or books. The Chinese people discovered more uses for this product. They started wrapping their medicines and other dried products in paper, instead of fabric. They also created paper lanterns and paper fans.

However, according to some records, when an event took place during winter, the Han dynasty did not have enough flowers to decorate the halls of the palace. The eunuchs and palace maids deceived the emperor and the nobles by adding paper flowers among the hundreds of real flowers. Because of its success, the dynasty started incorporating paper flowers with real ones to brighten their venues.

Paper flowers also became a tool of communication for rebellion. It was said that rebels would send flowers to a young girl, whose father was a member. It was to deceive the authorities by making them believe that it was a form of courtship. Even if they suspect the flowers to have a rebellious message, they could not prove it because the flowers easily dissolves in water with the message. Of course, for some people, the messages in the flowers were purely messages of love.

During the medieval period, the use of paper spread all over Europe. However, Europeans did not embrace paper flowers. They still used fabrics and metal flowers to should there be shortage of real flowers. Only the poor families used paper flowers in their homes.

The poor Europeans used paper flowers to replicate the flower accessories used in fashion. They made paper flower crowns instead of those made of fabric and silver.

The paper flowers slightly overtook the use of fabric and metal flowers in Europe during the First World War. It was because the supply of fabric and metals became limited. The women's fashion also changed. They started wearing smaller accessories.

Making small flowers using fabric and metals were difficult. However, papers were more flexible. People can create small paper flowers with ease by using the same patterns as the large paper flowers.

Paper flowers were set aside again after the discovery of the plastic in Europe. The plastic flowers were more economical because they can be kept and reused. The artificial flower industry in Europe boomed again.

Even today, paper flowers has not fully regained its status in the flower industry. Not many factories produce paper flowers. If a person wants to use paper flowers, they would have to make it on their own. No machines can mass produce paper flowers. They need to be delicately assembled by hands.

However, making paper flowers is a fairly simple process and only requires the simplest of materials. All you need to do is follow the guides we would be providing you with in the later chapters.

Reasons to Prefer Paper Flowers over Fresh Flowers

Using fresh flowers in an event is always the best option. However, there are some reasons and instances where paper flowers are better than fresh flowers. Here are some of them:

1. ***It gives more creative opportunities.*** Paper flowers are flexible. They do not need any season to grow, nor water to keep them vibrant. You can always create a flower of any color and of any kind. It presents you with lots of creative flexibility. You can create a hybrid of flowers to match your event or your motifs.

2. ***It is cheaper and more practical.*** Paper flowers are cheaper than most flowers and more practical to use. The most common paper used for the flowers are crepe papers which can be bought in any bookstore at a cheap price.

    You can also make the flowers weeks before your event without the fear that it might wither. You also do not run the risk of encountering unavailable stocks because of the season. This significantly lessens the number of things you need to worry about.

3. ***It is environment-friendly.*** Flowers are food for many animals, such as the butterflies and the bees. The more we use real fresh flowers, the more we deprive them of their food. Without the flowers, the food cycle of many animals would be affected. The ecology might become affected, too, if we keep using fresh flowers to decorate venues all the time.

On the other hand, the paper used for the paper flowers are often made from recycled paper pulp. The old paper flowers may also be recycled into new paper pulps. Thus, making the flowers would not produce any garbage. Instead, it will lessen it.

4. ***It is free from allergens.*** Paper flowers do not have pollen. They also attract less dust than plastic and metal flowers. If you place them in your home or venue for a long time, you will not attract any allergens that could ruin the event for any of your visitors.

Pests do not like them, too. You seldom see rats, cockroaches and other insects chewing on paper.

5. ***It is fun and easy to make.*** Most paper flowers are easy to make that you can turn it into a fun activity with your children or other members of your family.

In fact, during the Medieval age, some women from poor counties would come together to enjoy an afternoon of making paper flowers for their home.

There's no need for intricate steps and precise dimensions to create them. Only your patience and interest can limit the fun and creativity of the activity.

Chapter 2 – Equipment and Materials You Need for your Paper Flower Making Kit

During the ancient times, Chinese and Victorian women made their paper flowers with limited materials. Today, there are many materials and equipment that will help you create beautiful and wonderful paper flowers and accessories for your paper gardens. Here are some materials and equipment that you should keep on your paper flower making kit:

Basic Materials and Equipment
1. ***Paper.*** What is paper flower making without it? Any kind of paper can be used to make flowers. Most artists use crepe paper and construction paper. However, some serious artists use "washi" a variety of Japanese paper that is similar to crepe paper, but with sturdier and with better fibers.

2. ***Glue.*** Any glue or adhesive paste will do. In most types of paper flowers, you would only use a dab of glue at the beginning and in the end. A small bottle will go a long way.

For papers that require wires and other slippery materials, hot glue are used.

3. ***Scissors.*** Scissors are essential in paper flower making. It is used to cut delicate shapes of petals. The blunt side of the scissor is also used for curling the edges of the petals to make the flower appear to be in bloom.

Additional Materials and Equipment

The items listed below are not really required, but they will help you create more types of flowers.

1. **Strings.** Nylon, fabric or metal strings are sometimes used to bind the petals and the stems together. You can bind the petals with paper strips, too, but strings can hold them together better.

2. **Adhesive Tapes.** Adhesive tapes also work like the strings. They are more useful in holding the petals together. There are now colored adhesive tapes that are sold, usually in flower shops and art stores. You can use them to wrap the stems for better appearance

3. **Sticks.** Sticks are usually used for stems. Rolled papers are often used for the stems. But, you can use thin metal rods for better flexibility.

4. **Rulers.** Regular rulers are helpful when cutting uniform cuts in your paper. It would also be helpful if you have a small French ruler. It will help in creating perfect curves for your petals.

5. **Wires.** For flowers that are too small for you to use the sticks, or those that have to be bent, flexible wires are used instead of wooden or paper sticks.

Basic Parts of a Paper Flower

Petals

Petals make the flower. In paper flowers, the creation of petals is the most important step. The beauty of your flower will depend on how you formed, shaped and curled the petals.

Each flower has different types of petal. Some flowers would have a single wide petal, while some, like the daisies would have plenty of petals. The steps of making the petal would vary with each flower.

Center of the Flower

The center of the petal is made up of three parts.

1. *Stigma.* In most paper flowers, only the stigma could be seen. This is usually the round part that collects the petal. Stigma is a must for each flower to highlight the petals.

2. *Style.* The style is the cord that lifts the stigma. It is essential in some flowers, like the calla lily.

3. *Anther and filament.* Paper flowers usually do not include these parts, but you might have to include this if you are making big flowers.

4. *Sepal.* This part is the set of leaves that cover the gathering point of the petals. It is also a must for flowers that might be placed on a stand or vase.

Stem

It is the long stick that holds the flowers up. It is essential when you are creating bouquet of flowers or standing flowers decorations.

Leaves

Leaves might be necessary for long-stemmed stalk flowers. There are also some flowers that require at least a leaf to complete the look.

Chapter 3 - Origami and Kirigami Paper Flowers

Origami Paper Flowers

Origami Paper flowers are made by folding the flowers in a particular pattern. They need less cutting and gluing. They are usually used as wall decorations. These types of paper flowers are good and safe for kids. However, they are delicate. When you make a mistake, you might have to start from the beginning. It is also a good choice of paper flowers, if you intend to reuse the papers for other projects.

The materials you need to make these flowers are only papers. Glue might be used, if you want to make the folds permanent.

Traditional Origami Flower

Material:

- 4 x 4 construction or any colored paper.

Directions:

1. Fold the paper diagonally to the right to make a wide triangle. Unfold. Do the same in the other direction. Your paper will have a wide, equal "X".

2. Fold the paper vertically in the middle to make a tall rectangle. Unfold.

3. Fold the paper horizontally in the middle to make a wide rectangle. Your paper will now have an "X" and "+".

4. Join the 2 lines of the left lower quadrant of the "+". Push the center line to the center

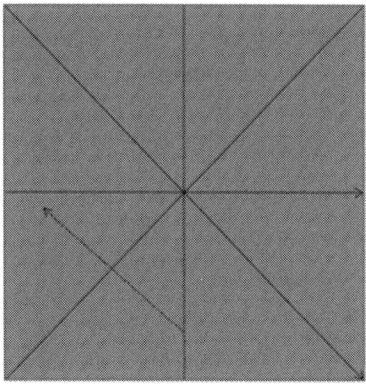

5. The center line of the quadrant will produce a triangle below. Then Fold the center line of the upper right quadrant to the center line of the lower quadrant.

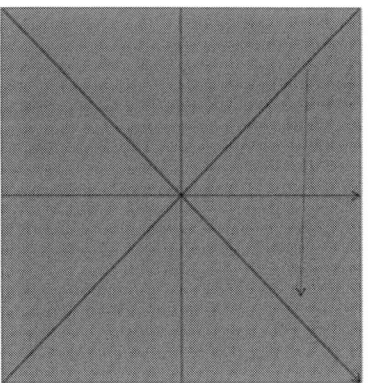

6. Fold the 2 lines of the right quadrant. You will end up with a smaller square, which is a quarter of the original size. Below the tops square are 2 triangles. Press the lines of the new square to make it easier for you to fold.

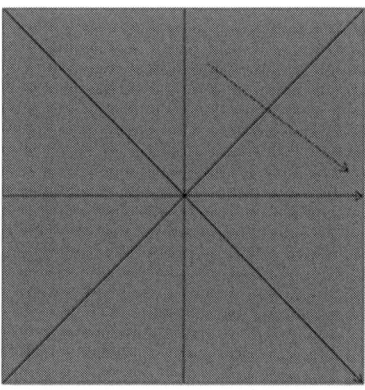

7. Lift the lower triangle and push

8. Raise one side of the top square. You will have a vertical or standing triangle at the center.

9. Press the top line of the triangle to the center and flatten the sides.

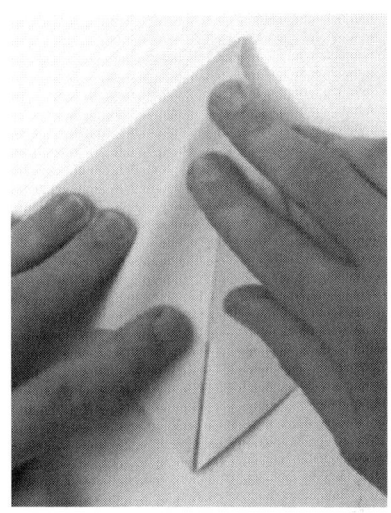

10. Flip the right side of the triangle over the left triangle. You will end with a square with 3 triangles on the lower portion – 2 small triangles stacked against each other and a wider triangle.

11. Fold the wider triangle under the upper triangle.

12. Flip the other half of the triangle into a vertical triangle again and repeat step 8 and 9. Do the same with the remaining big triangles.

13. You will end up with continuous diamonds and broken diamonds.

Figure 1. Continuous

Figure 2. Broken

14. Fold all the lower part of the continuous diamond.

15. Arrange the triangles so you will end up with a stack of big and small triangle on each side.

16. Fold the triangle in the middle. Fold the pointed part to the left side, to make a smaller triangle.

17. Push the middle of the smaller triangle towards the inside. The shape will look like the head of the origami pigeon.

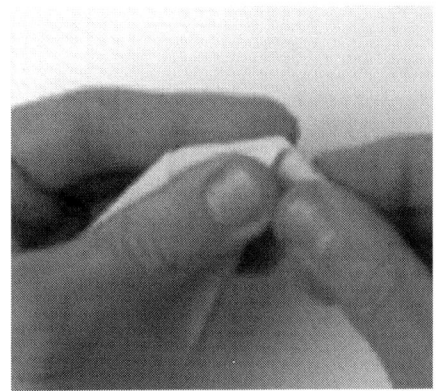

18. Unfold the point and hold tightly. Spread the upper portion of the paper. You will end up with a flower with star petals. You can leave them that way for a star flower or you can push the fold between the petals to make a wide, curved petal.

2-Piece Traditional Origami Flower

This traditional origami flower is made of two parts. The parts should be joined to create a flower. It may have the same form as the first origami flower, but it will be thicker and have more defined lines.

Materials: 2 pieces of 4" x 4" paper, preferably of the same color.

Directions:

1. Follow steps 1 to 6 of the traditional origami flower.

2. With your little square, push the edges towards the middle to create a big and small triangle. See illustration below:

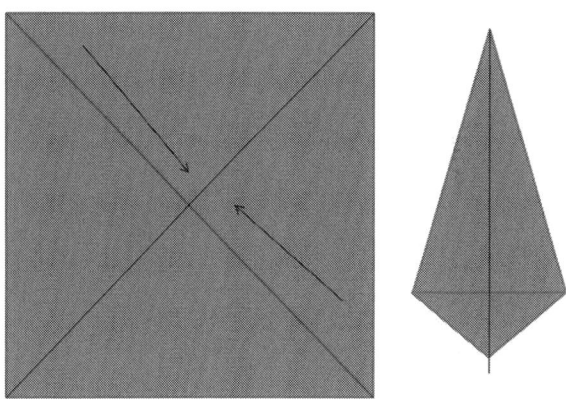

3. Unfold the paper. Then, refold it into a triangle

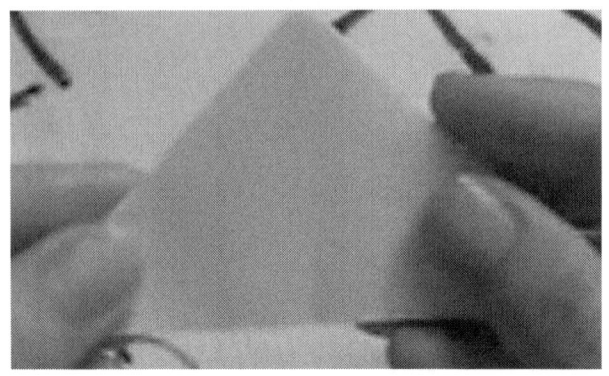

4. Lift the center line of the triangle. Press the lower right edge to the top right edge to create a smaller triangle. Then, fold the left triangle over to the right. Do the same to the other triangles. See the instructions below:

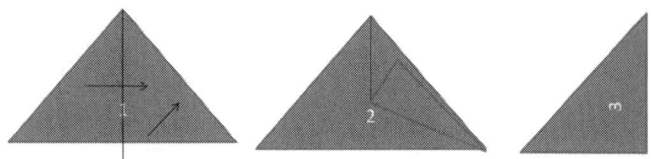

5. Open the triangle. You will have 2 middle triangles. If you look it flatly, your paper will look this way:

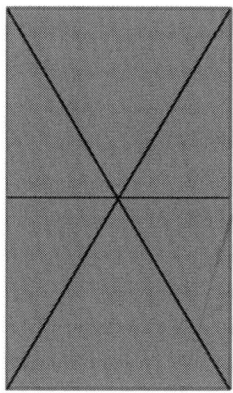

6. Push the side down and fold to connect the top and low points of the two sides together. Press tightly to have a definite four-petal star.

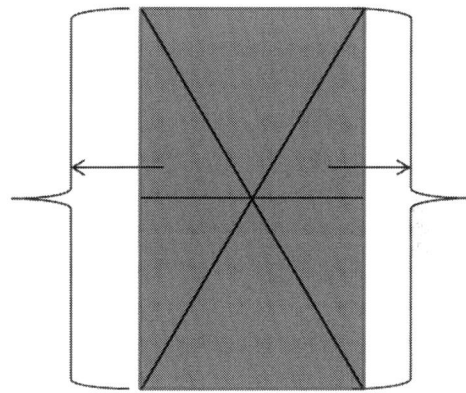

7. Press the petals together. There should be 2 pointy petals on both sides.

8. Open the center of the petals and press it flat to create a wider petal. Curl the tip of

the petal to give it more details, just like this picture below:

9. Create another set of petals using the other paper.

10. Join the two sets of petals into one flower, just like this:

Origami Rosettes

Materials: 4 x 4 paper, construction paper is preferred

Direction:

1. Repeat steps 1 to 3 of the traditional origami flowers.

2. Align the horizontal line of the "+" towards the center. Then, align the vertical line. You will end up with 2 equal triangles, with folded triangles in between.

3. Fold the point of the two sides of the triangle to the top point. Do the same with the other side. You will end up with a smaller square, with folded triangles on top.

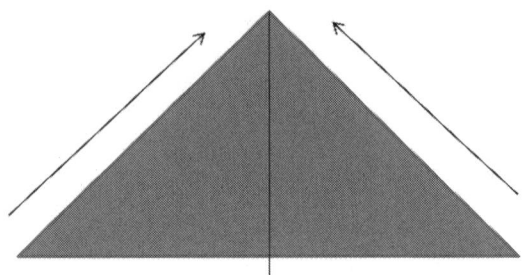

4. Fold the top part of the left triangles to the lower point. Do the same with the right side.

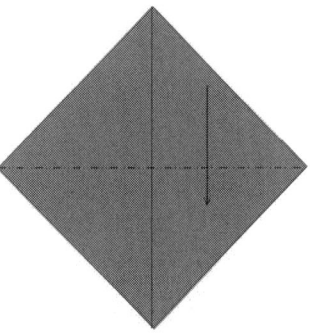

5. Unfold the left top triangle. Open the fold and push the center to make a small box. Do the same to the other three triangles. You will end with the same figure as below.

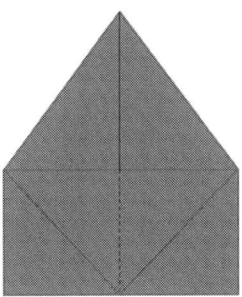

6. Fold the top triangle towards the center point.

7. Open the folded parts of the rectangle. Press center folds towards the middle to make two opposite triangles. You will obtain this figure.

8. Flip the paper. You will have a big triangle in the middle with four foldable boxes. Spread the middle part of the big triangle. Do not flatten it. Shape it like an "8".

9. Pinch the middle portion of the "8" and twist it as hard as you can. The rest of the folds will follow and form curves around the area.

10. Roll the sharp edges of the petals using a pen or a barbecue stick to curve and shape the flowers.

Cherry Blossom

Materials:

- 4 x 6 paper of any type and color
- Scissors

Directions:

1. Fold the paper horizontally to make a wide rectangle. Fold the rectangle again horizontally in half. Unfold to the wider rectangle again.

2. Take the left lower endpoint of the rectangle and fold it towards the center. Unfold. You will have a paper with and "x" on one side, but a plain box on the other.

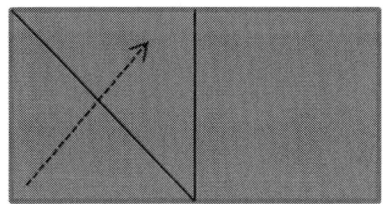

3. Fold the upper right endpoint of the right rectangle towards the center of the "x" in left square.

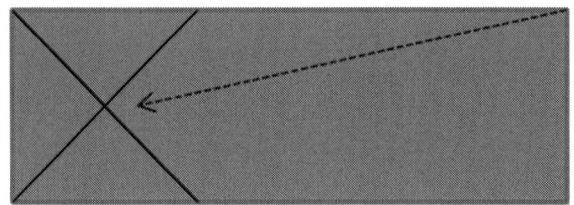

4. Take the endpoint from the center of the x and fold it towards the border of the right rectangle to create a triangle.

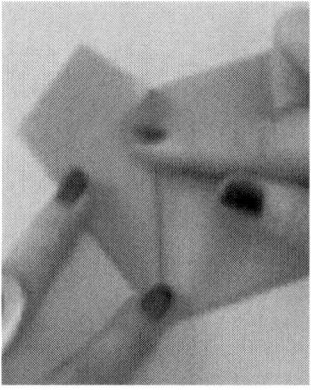

5. Fold the left part of the rectangle to make another triangle. Now you have 2 triangles. One of the triangles will be wider than the first one.

6. Fold the two triangles against each other. The left triangle should be below the right one.

7. Cut the folded triangles in equal length. Cut a small left diagonal portion of the

right edge of the triangle. Then, cut a curve line from the new point towards the center line, a few centimeters below the top point. See the picture below.

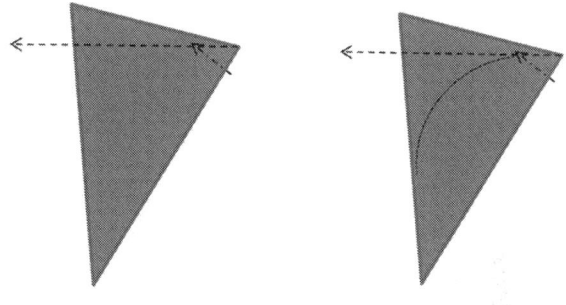

8. Open the paper. You will end with five petals with a small "v" on the top part.

9. Fold the petals inward, until you will have stacked petals. Make sure that the right side has three folds, while the left only has two folds.

10. Fold the edge of the side with two stacks towards you. The fold should be about 10mm. Flip the petal and fold the side with three stacks towards you.

11. Open the flower. Define the folds of the edges to make the flower stand out.

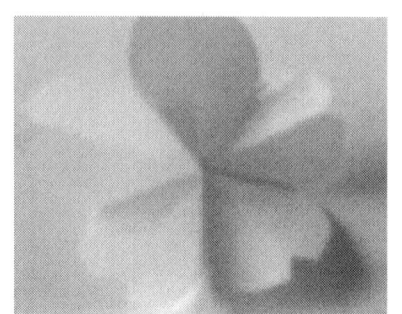

Five Petal Flower

Material:

- 5 pieces 2" x 2" piece of paper
- Glue

Direction:

1. Fold the paper in half, diagonally.
2. Pull the edges of the paper to the center line to form 2 triangles. See picture below:

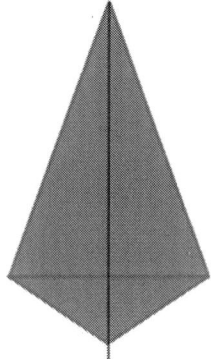

3. Fold the lower triangle over. Unfold the piece.
4. Fold the lower triangle again.

5. Pull the sides of the edges of the lower triangle to the center. You will end up with a square and an inverted "L" trapezoid on the right side and on top.

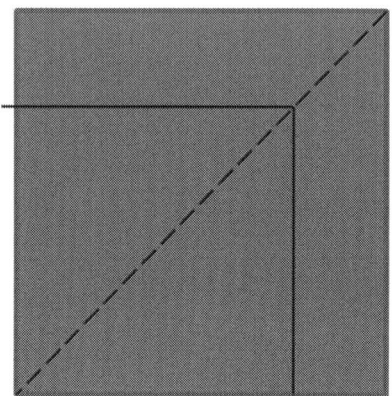

6. Fold the paper to the outside to create a triangle. Unfold the top trapezoid.

7. Fold the right bottom point over to the top point. Press the fold to create a guide. Insert the right bottom point inside the top triangle. You will end up with a shape similar to an envelope.

8. Fold the bottom edges towards the center line. The left part of the envelope will look uneven.

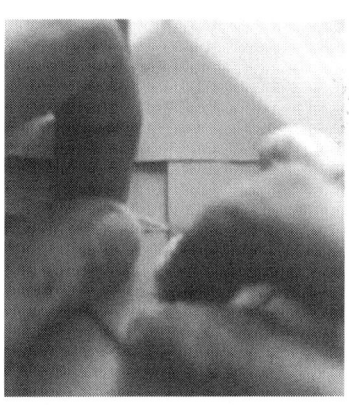

9. Raise the right part up and push to the left side. Take the right edge of the lower trapezoid and press to the middle. You will have three sections. The left side, the center triangle and the right side. The left and right side will have 2 triangles at the top and bottom.

10. Gather the parts together and open the division at the bottom of the center

triangle. This will be one of the petals. Make 4 other petals.

11. Place glue on the bottom half of the petal and connect the other petal.

12. After you glued all the petals. Place glue on the bottom part of the last petal and pull it over to the first petal to form a star flower.

Tip: You can add more petals to make 8 or 12 petal flowers. However, you may need to place a stigma at the center.

Paper Fan Flowers

Among the origami flowers, this might be the easiest to do. Even little kids can do it. Here are three ways of making it:

Method 1:

In this method, you will not need any decoration at the center.

Materials:

- 2 pieces of 4"x4" paper
- 2 pieces of 2" by 2" paper (should be a different color than the bigger-sized papers)
- Glue

Directions:

1. Fold the paper in half. Do not unfold.

2. Fold it again to make 4 quarters. Continue folding it until you get at least 8 folds. Unfold.

3. Crease the paper, using the folds as a guide, in an inward-outward motion. You will end up with a paper accordion

4. Gather the accordion strip together and fold in half. Stick the sides of the centerfold to hold the shape. You will now end up with a paper fan. Do the same with the other piece of paper.

5. Stick the two fans together to create a full circle.

6. Repeat steps 1 to 6 on the smaller size paper. This will be your center.

7. Place the smaller flower on the center of the big flower. Arrange the petals so that the smaller petals fit in into the creases of the larger flower.

Method 2:

This is only a short cut of method 1. However, it will not give you the two-layer effect.

Directions:

1. Paste the smaller paper to the center of the larger paper. Make sure that the distances on the edges are equal.

2. Repeat steps 2 to 5 of Method 1.

Method 3:

Materials:

- 3 pieces of 2" x 6" paper of the same color.
- Glue
- Button, or any cardboard

Directions:

1. Fold the paper like an accordion. Make sure that the creases are equal. Do the same with the other papers.

2. Gather and glue the ends of the accordion strips.

3. Join the ends of the strip to create a circle. Set the loose flower on the table.

4. Gather the bottom ends to the center.

5. Measure the size of the center. You can just eyeball it.

6. Cut a circle or a flower shape. Place enough glue on one side.

7. Press the center to the gathered accordion strip. While the glue is still wet, arrange the petals. Leave the glue to dry.

8. At this point, you can leave the flower on that side. However, if you want to hang it or make it more dimensional, you can repeat step 6 and 7 to the other side of the flower.

Tulip

Materials: 6" x 6" paper, any color or type, but for beginners, construction paper is advised.

Direction:

1. Fold your paper diagonally on each side to have an "X" marking on the paper.

2. Fold your papers vertically and horizontally to have a "+" marking.

3. Press the horizontal folds towards the center to deduce your paper into 2 stacked triangles, with the flaps on the side.

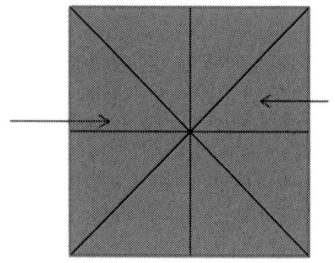 

4. Inver the triangle to make the point going towards you. Connect the two end points to the center and fold to create a small diamond. Flip the paper and do the same on the other side.

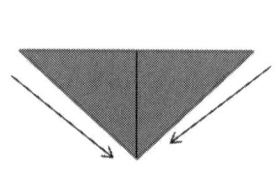 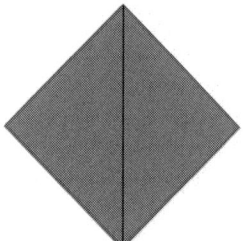

5. Turn the paper upside down again, so all the opening would be on top.

6. Flip the pages of the diamond to find a page where there is no opening.

7. Fold the top edges of the diamond towards the center line. You will end up with this shape again:

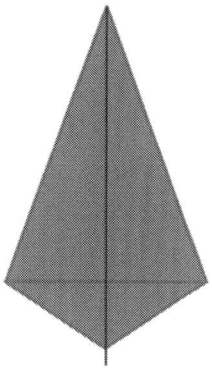

8. Unfold the triangles from the center. Then, fold the left triangle to the middle of the right triangle. Fold the right triangle over to the left triangle. Flip the paper and do the other side.

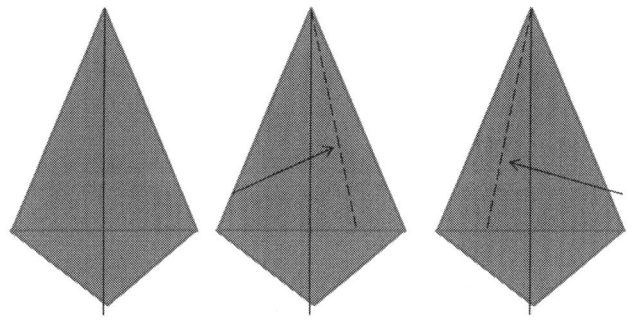

9. Now, you will have a paper with this appearance:

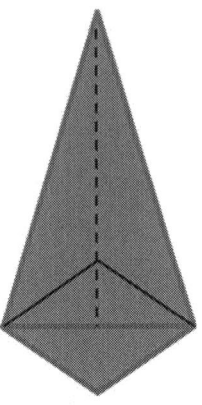

10. Open the pocket of the left triangle and insert the right triangle. Do the same on the other side.

11. Open the pockets at the bottom of the triangle. Tear a small hole on the bottom point and blow to inflate the flower.

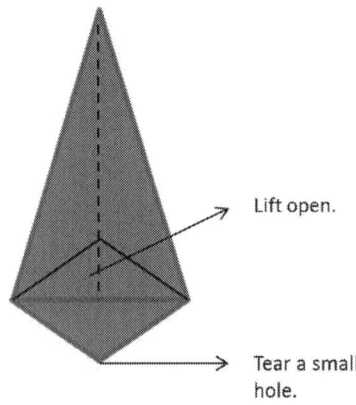

12. Fold the petals of the flower to the outside.

13. Wrap a stick with green paper and insert it the hole. You can also create your own origami stem and leaf. Here's how:

    a. Get an 8" by 8" green paper.

    b. Make a diamond by folding all the edges to the center.

    c. Fold the bottom of diamond towards the center again. You will end up with a narrower diamond.

    d. Join the top and the bottom point. You will notice that the bottom part will not cover the whole top.

    e. Slowly pull the two points away from each other. The inner part will be the stem. Insert the point of the stem to the hole at the bottom of the flower.

    f. Open up the outer side of the paper to create an impression of a leaf.

Lily

https://www.shutterstock.com/image-photo/origami-lily-model-isolated-on-white-533071075?src=ZmM_YMqqhJWVk0firTustg-1-8

Materials: 1 piece of 6" by 6" construction paper

Direction:

1. Make the primary folds by folding diagonally to create the "x" crease and by folding perpendicularly to create the "+" mark."

2. Fold the horizontal lines towards the center to make 2 triangles. Make sure that the side can be flipped.

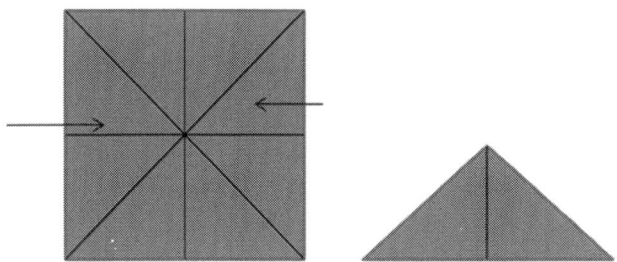

3. Flip the left flap up and flap over to the right. Unfold the flap and keep it in a vertical position, like a shark fin. Open the fin and press the center. Keep the center line of the triangle pressed down. Open the left flap and press the center to create a triangle. Flip your paper and do the same to the other side.

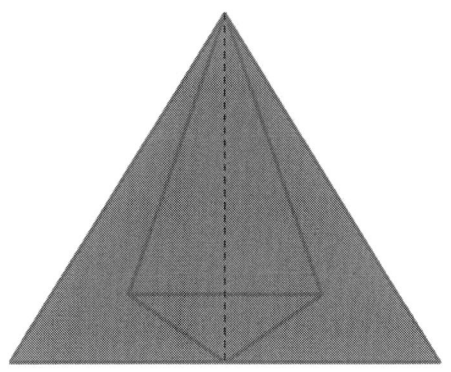

4. Fold the small triangles at the center and push it to the left. This will raise the right flap. Repeat step 3 for the other flaps. You will end with 4 stacks of diamond-shaped paper.

5. Open and divide the flaps equally on both sides.

6. Rotate your paper to 180 degrees, with the point facing to the right.

7. Fold the top flap of the left triangle towards the centerline. Do the same with the bottom flap. Flip your paper and do the same to the other side. Do the same with the other 2 sides.

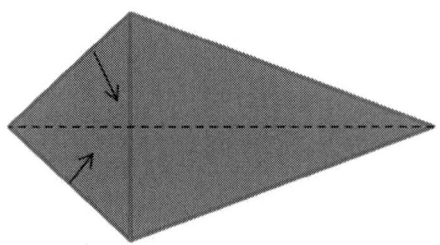

8. Unfold all the folds you made in step 7 and fold the paper by connecting the two end points together. Unfold. Flip your paper and fold to the end points again. Unfold.

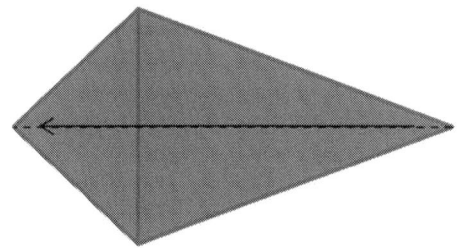

9. Flip your paper to 90 degrees. Lift one of the bottom flaps and push the top part towards the top point. Flatten the rest to make a smaller diamond. See the picture below. Turn your paper over and do the other sides.

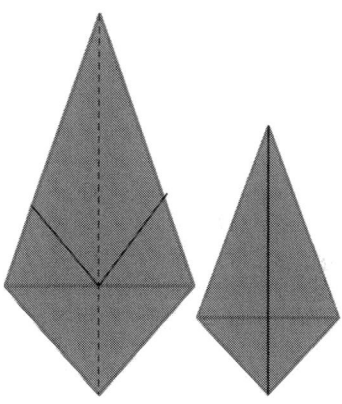

10. Open the top part of the flower and fold down. It would look like a tall and perfect diamond, just like the picture. Flip your paper and do the same to the other side. Open the side part of your paper and repeat the same steps.

The bottom of your diamond should have four flaps.

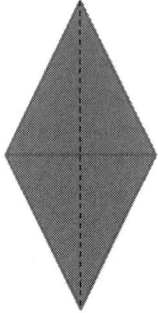

11. Turn your paper to 180 degrees. The flaps should point to the right.

12. Fold the edges of left portion of the diamond towards the centerline. Turn your paper over and repeat the step. Open the sides of your paper and do the same steps to all sides.

13. Turn your paper by 90 degrees to the left. Your diamond will be uneven again. The bottom part will have the longer triangle and all the flaps should be on the top.

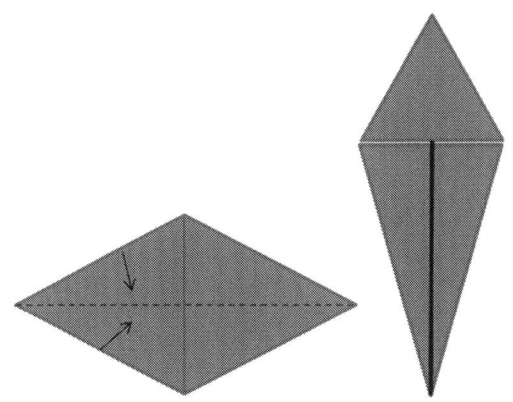

14. Pull one of the flaps away from the center to expose the inside of the flower. Place a pencil or and round stick over it. Roll the flap towards you to curl the petals. Do the same with the other flaps.

15. You can tear a little hole on the bottom part of your flowers to stick your stem. Note: The leaf and stem used for the tulip may also be used for this flower.

Kusudama (Modular Origami)

Materials:

- 5 piece 3" by 3" construction or origami paper
- *Glue*
- *Round bead, optional*

Directions:

1. Fold your paper diagonally. Turn it over so the base of the triangle is facing towards you.

2. Take the bottom left point of the triangle and connect it to the top point. The left base should meet the centerline. Do the

same with the right side. You will end up with a square with two triangles on top.

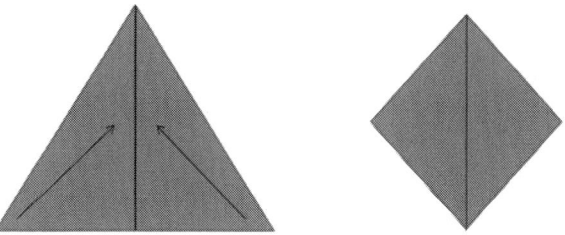

3. Fold the 2 triangles to the outside in half. Your paper would look like this:

4. Lift the right triangle up. Expand it and press it flat. Do the same with the left triangle.

5. Turn your paper over. You will have a square and the edges of your triangles. Tuck the point of the diamond to the inside, under the square. Turn your paper over again and you will have this:

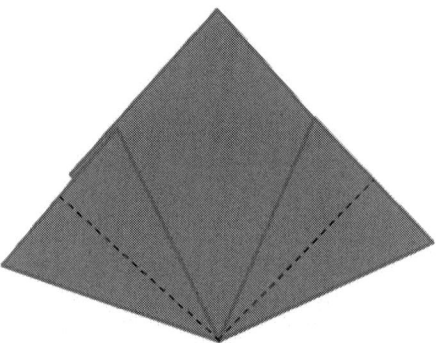

6. Fold the outer triangles inside along the center crease. You will end with a rhombus

with two thin triangles on the lower edges. Glue the two thin triangles together. See the diagram.

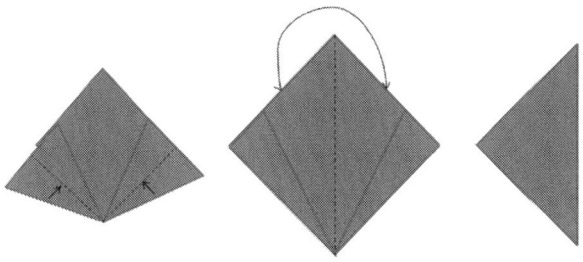

7. Open the triangle to show the details inside.

8. Repeat all the steps with the other pieces of papers.

9. Connect one side of the triangle with another until you form a star petal.

10. Curl the top tip of the petals a little. Add a bead at the center of the flower, if desired.

Kirigami Paper Flowers

Kirigami is a deviation of origami. It also involves paper folding, but the paper used is already cut in certain pattern to create the desired outcome.

These types of flowers are formed by cutting a single paper into a flower. They are often used in wallpapers, scrapbooks and as a flat decoration. For this type, you only need to do very minimal cutting. You usually cut only one side, but the flower will have uniform petals and edges.

Carnation

Materials: 1 piece 4" x 4" paper

Directions:

1. Fold the paper diagonally to form an "X". Fold it again in half to make a triangle. Fold the triangle at the crease to make a smaller triangle.

2. Fold the right side of the triangle over the center of the left side. Fold the remaining portion of the left side over the right side.

3. Cut the tail, so you will be left with a perfect isosceles triangle.

4. Flip the folded paper, so the base will be on top and the point is towards you.

5. 1/4 from the point, draw a small "V" in the middle, about 1/3 of the height of the triangle. Draw a concave half-circle on top of the right diagonal line. Make sure that the point of the concave touches the edge of the triangle.

6. At least 1/3 from the top of your paper, draw a curve line from the right edge of the triangle towards the left point of the "V".

7. Draw a larger curve above the curve lines. The second curve will touch the edge of the triangle, near the "V". This will make your outline look thicker.

8. From the middle of the top curve line, draw another curve upward to the left edge, about ¼ from the top of the paper. Draw another line under it, with the same thickness as the rest of the outline.

9. The pattern would look like this:

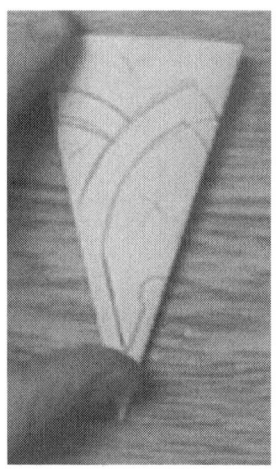

10. Cut by tracing the outer lines at the top of your paper.

11. Cut the space under the second outline and along the "V" and the half circle. If you can see it from the pictures, you should cut all the parts with the "x" sign.

12. Slowly unfold the paper and you will end with a 12-petal outline of a carnation flower.

8-Petal Kirigami Flower

Material: 1 piece 6"x 6" colored construction paper

Directions:

1. Fold the paper in half, diagonally.

2. Fold the triangle in half. Then, fold the smaller triangle in half.

3. Hold the paper in a position where the flaps are away from you and the point is towards you.

4. Draw a design at the center of the folded paper. You can do any design, but make sure that you do not cut the paper all the way to the corners. Try this design below. Just cut the area noted as "x".

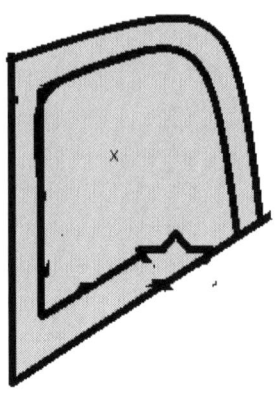

Note, if you want to have narrower and pointy petals, you can follow steps 1 to 3 of the carnation for the initial folds.

Chapter 4 – Long Strip Paper Flowers

3D Paper Flowers

3D paper flowers often look like real flowers from afar. They also would have intricate details, which might make you think that they are difficult to do. Making 3D paper flowers is actually even easier than origami and kirigami paper flowers. It has lesser steps. However, they might involve a lot of cutting and gluing. You might have to use different colors of paper, too.

In this chapter, you will find the different steps in making paper flowers using long strips of papers for petals and leaves.

Daisy

Materials:

- 1 piece of 6" x 1.5" strip of paper
- 1 piece of 6" x ¼" strip of paper, must be darker than the wider paper. Yellow, orange and red are often used.
- Small, flat brown or yellow bead
- Glue
- Scissors
- Thin stick, not more than ¼" in diameter, for the stem (optional)
- Dark green paper, for the stem (optional)

Directions:

1. Take the thin strip of paper. Roll it from the tip to the end, in order to make a thick

round stigma. Gradually glue the strip as you roll to keep it secure.

If you are adding a stem, roll the thin strip around the tip of the stem. Make sure to wrap your stem in green paper before doing this.

2. Take the wider strip of paper. Draw a horizontal line ½" inch from the top. Fold the paper to make a crease.

3. Cut the lower part of the paper, vertically, into thin strips. Do not cut behind the top line. Make the strips uniform as possible. See the diagram below.

4. Close your scissor tightly. Using the blunt side of the scissor, curl the thin strips outward, slightly.

5. Invert the paper, so that the strips are away from you.

6. Add glue on one side of the uncut portion of the paper. Attach it to the stigma.

7. Roll the petals to the stigma. Glue the strip as you roll.

8. You can leave the flower as it is, or you can put a bead at the center to highlight the stigma.

9. If you are using a stem, cut a short strip of green paper (about 4" by 1"). Wrap it over the joining part of the flower and the stem to create the sepal.

Calendula

Paper Calendula is made the same way as the ordinary daisy, but it has trickier steps in assembling the petals and the stigma.

Materials:

- 2 pieces of 1" x 6" strip of paper (different colors, one should be lighter)
- 1 piece 1.5" x 4" strip of paper, green color
- 1 piece of 1.5" x 7" strip of paper, must be the same color as the lighter strip.
- 1 piece of 2" x 8" strip of paper. It can be the same color as the lighter strip or a darker shade.
- Glue
- Scissors
- Thin stick, not more than ¼" in diameter, for the stem (optional)
- Dark green paper, for the stem 3" by 18" strip (optional)

Directions:

1. Take the dark colored 1" x 6" strip of paper. Fold it horizontally in half.

2. Cut the other half into thin strips. The thinner you cut, the better.

3. Roll the strip into a round stigma, just like in step 1 of the daisy paper flower. Make sure not to glue the strips. Set aside.

4. Take the other 1" x 6" strip. Fold it vertically in half. Fold it again thrice.

5. Measure ¼ inch from the top. Mark it with a line. At the other end, draw a curve line. Fold the top line to make a crease.

6. Cut the curve line. Cut also the creases on the sides, but only below the ¼ inch line.

7. Repeat steps 4 to 6 with the other strip of papers.

8. Unfold the 1" by 6". Using the blunt side of the scissors, curl the petals inward.

9. Attach the petals to the stigma. Apply the glue as you roll. Do not worry if the petal covers the thin strips of the stigma.

10. Get the 1.5" by 7" strip and curl the petals inward. Attach to the stigma.

11. Get the 2" by 8" strip and curl the petals outward and glue to the stigma.

12. Get the 1.5" x 4" green strip. Fold it in half, horizontally. Then, fold it vertically thrice.

13. Cut a concave curve on the top half of the green strip. See below:

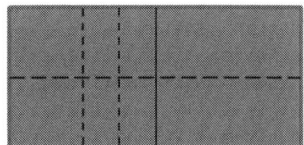  

14. Unfold. If you are not using a stem, attach the strip on the last layer of the flower. Leave half of the uncut part hanging from the stigma. Place glue at the bottom of the flower and fold the hanging part to cover the bottom.

15. If you are adding a stem, do the following steps:

    a. Get the strip for the stem.

    b. Fold it until you deduce it to around 2" to 3".

    c. Mark ½ inch at the top part of the strip.

    d. Draw curve lines on the edges.

    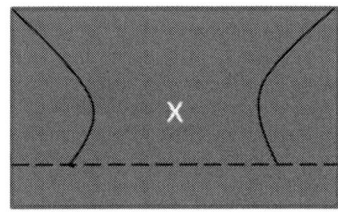

    e. Cut the part mark with x. Unfold.

    f. Glue the stem to the bottom of your paper. You can use hot glue to secure it better. Secure the hanging part of the sepal to the stem.

    g. Wrap the connecting part of the stems with the leaves twice until it is fully covered. Then, attach the rest of the strip on the stick in a downward direction.

Lavender

Materials:

- Crepe papers, violet and green
- Stick, about ¼ inch thick and 6" tall
- Glue
- Scissors
- Permanent marker, blue, yellow or violet

Direction:

1. Cut a long strip of violet crepe papers with the width of 1.5". Fold the strip to around 5" long.

2. Draw a horizontal line on top of the paper, about ¼ inch from the top edge of the paper.

3. Draw strips of about ½ wide on the paper. Then, draw a curve the edge of the paper. Place a thick dot at the center of the curves. Cut the curve lines, up to the horizontal line. Unfold and set aside.

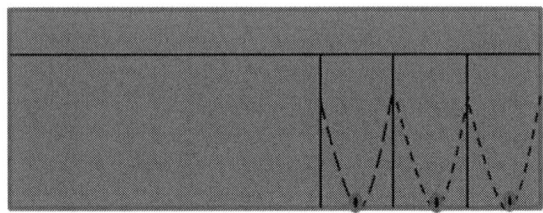

4. Cut a long strip of green paper about .5" wide. Wrap the strip neatly around your stick.

5. Roll out the petal strip. Curl the petals outward. Wrap the top of the stem with the petals twice. Carefully move the strip away from the top petals by about half inch. Roll the strip twice on the spot before moving down by another inch. Continue repeating the steps until you reach the ¾ mark of the stick. Cut the excess strip and set aside.

6. Cut a long strip of green paper, about 2.5" in width.

7. Repeat step 3, but do not place the dot at the center of the curves.

8. Unfold and curve the leaves inward.

9. From the last row of the violet petals, roll the leaves around twice. Move down by ¼ inch and roll the leaves twice again. Cut the extra strip.

10. Wrap the ends with another roll of green strip of paper.

Simple Rose

There are many ways when making a simple rose using long strips of paper. Here are some of them:

Method 1:
Materials:

- 1 piece 4" by 4" construction paper
- 1 piece 1" by 1" construction paper, preferably color green
- Glue
- Small bead, optional

Direction:

1. Take the 4" x 4" paper and divide the area to 16 1-inch cubes. You can either draw it with pencil or fold it.
2. Draw an outline of a spiral, starting from the center of the paper. See the picture for reference:

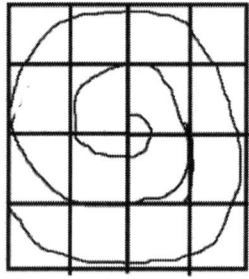

3. Cut along the spiral lines. Discard the excess paper.
4. Roll the paper to form a small tube starting from the center of the spiral strip. Hold the bottom end tightly with your fingers. Apply glue at the bottom of the tube.
5. Roll a wider layer, about ½ inch away from the center. Gather the bottom part and glue it to the bottom of the tube.
6. Apply glue at the bottom of the tube again.
7. Repeat step 5, until you reach the end of the strip.
8. Take the 1" by 1" paper. Cut it in a circle. Curl the edges slightly. Apply glue at the bottom of your rose and attach the rose.

Note: If you want to add a stem, you can do the following:

1. Wrap a stick with brown or green paper. Apply glue on the tip and attach the rose.
2. You may also roll the green paper into a hard rod and use as a stem.

Method 2

Materials:

- Crepe papers, green and other colors
- Glue
- Stick, optional for stem

Direction:

1. Cut 2 long strips of crepe paper with 2" width.

2. Fold one of the strips until you get a square of 2 inches.

3. Fold the other one until you get a 1.5" by 2" rectangle.

4. Draw a horizontal line at the bottom of the papers, about ½ inch away from the bottom edge. Draw an arc on the top of the paper.

Make a crease at the horizontal line of the 2" square.

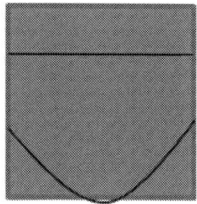

5. Roll out the 2 sets of petals.

6. Take the 1.5" size petal. Using the blunt side of the scissor, curl the petals outward.

7. Take one end of the strip. Roll the first petal into a slim tube. Apply glue at the bottom part.

8. Cover the rolled first petal with the second petal. Glue the bottom part together.

9. Cover the previous layer with 2 petals.

10. Repeat step 9 twice.

11. Cover the preceding layer with three petals. Repeat the step twice, too. Arrange the petals, so that it will not be stacked against each other.

12. The next layers should be 4 petals and the succeeding 2 layers should be 5 petals.

13. Cut the excess paper.

14. Take the wider strip of petals. Curb the petals upward using the blunt side of the scissors again. Start from the crease to the top.

15. Cover the previous layer with 5 petals twice.

16. The next two layers should be covered with 7 petals. At this point, you can cut the excess strip of paper. If you want to make your rose bloom larger, add more layers but, add 2 or 3 more petals on each layer.

Peony

Materials:

- Crepe paper, 3 shades of the same color
- Construction paper, same shade as the darkest shade of the crepe paper
- Green construction paper
- Glue
- Scissors

Directions:

1. Prepare the stigma by doing the following:

    a. Cut 3 pieces 4" by 1" of the dark-colored construction paper.

    b. Cut 1 piece of 8" by 2" of the dark-colored construction paper.

2. Take 1 piece of the 4" by 1" strip and roll it into a cylinder.

3. Get the other piece and fold it horizontally. Make thin fringes on the bottom half of the paper. Cut the paper into two.

4. Roll one half of the fringed paper to the top half of the cylinder.

5. Get the last 4" by 1" strip and roll it to the stigma. Glue it below the line of the fringes.

6. Take the other half of the fringed paper and roll it to the last layer. Again, glue it only to the top half of the cylinder.

7. Take the 8" by 2" strip. Draw a horizontal line, about 3/4 inch from the top edge. Fold to make a crease.

8. Draw vertical lines at the bottom of the line, just like when you make the petal for the daisy.

9. Curb the fringes inward using a stick or the blunt side of your scissor.

10. Roll the strip around the stigma. Make sure that the bottom is aligned with the center tube.

11. Prepare the petals by doing the following:

a. Cut a long strip of crepe paper with the width of 3 inches.

b. Cut a long strip of crepe paper with the width of 4 inches

c. Cut 2 long strips of crepe paper with 6 inches.

12. Take the 3-inch paper. Fold it until you have a 1" by 3" rectangle.

13. Take the 4-inch paper and fold it until you have a 1" by 4" rectangle.

14. Get one of the 6-inch crepe paper and fold it until you have a 1.5" by 6". Do the same with the other 6-inch paper, but make the rectangle into a 2" by 6".

15. At the bottom edge of the paper, draw a top part of a heart. It will look like this:

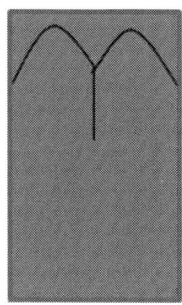

16. Unfold and curl the petals inward except for the 2" by 6" strip.

17. Pinch the middle of the petals to emphasize the detail of the petal.

18. Roll the 3" strip around the stigma. Make sure that the bottom is leveled. Do about 2 to 3 layers around the stigma. Cut the excess paper.

19. Continue rolling the 4" strip. Do 3 layers.

20. Use the 6" by 1.5" strip to make the next 3 layers.

21. Get the last strip of petals. Unfold and curl the petals outward.

22. Roll it behind the previous layers. Do two to 3 layers.

23. Prepare the sepal by doing the following:

    a. Cut one 8"by 4" strip of green paper.

    b. Fold it until you get a 1.5" by 4" rectangle.

    c. Draw a line, about 1-inch from the bottom edge. Fold to make a strong crease, enough that the paper would not spring back.

d. Draw an outline of a leaf on the top part. You can try doing a simple pattern like this:

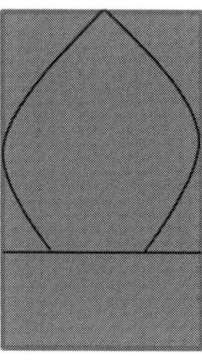

e. Cut the leaf part.

f. Wrap the strip around the flower.

Note: If you have a stem, attach the flower on the tip using hot glue. Cover with extra green paper or crepe paper.

Narcissus or Daffodil

Materials:

- Crepe paper, preferably one color of different shades
- Glossy paper from a magazine
- Thin stick
- Glue
- Scissors

Directions:

1. Cut a thin strip of about 6" by 1/2" inch of the darkest shade paper.

2. Roll it into a compact round cylinder.

3. Cut another strip of the same colored paper with a size of 1" by 4".

4. Make a horizontal crease, ½ inch from the bottom of the paper. Make tiny frills above the crease.

5. Add the frilled strip to the cylinder. Set aside.

6. Cut 6" by 2" of the lighter colored crepe paper. Make a ½" horizontal crease from the top edge of the paper.

7. Frill the ½" edge. Curl the fringes upward.

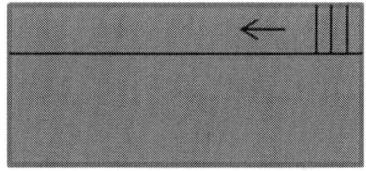

8. Apply glue on the bottom end of the strip. Attach it to the stigma.

9. Apply glue on the next portion of the stigma. Gather the bottom edge of the petal to make a short ruffle, about ½ inch.

10. Apply glue on the next portion again and attach the next ½" portion of the petal. Do not create a ruffle.

11. Repeat Step 9. Alternate it with step 10 until you complete two layers. Discard the excess paper.

12. Cut a long strip, with the width of 2.5 inches. You may use the darkest or the lightest crepe paper

13. Fold the paper until you have a stack of 6 2.5" by 2.5" square.

14. Draw an arc on the top part of the paper. Cut the arc portion.

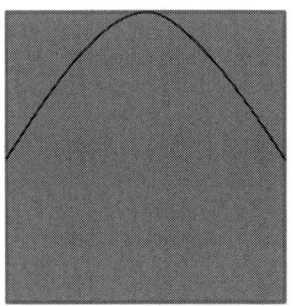

15. Fold the paper in the middle to make a vertical crease. Cut the crease, but leave about ¾ inch allowance at the bottom.

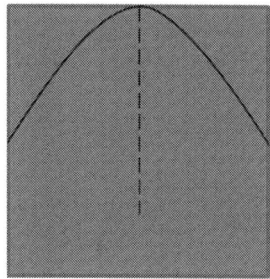

16. Unfold the petals.

17. Glue the cut portion of the petals together to about ¼ inch from the edge. This will give the petal a vertical scalloped curve.

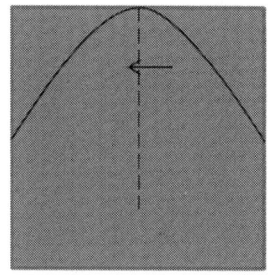

18. Attach the petal strip below the first layer of petals.

19. To make the stem, cut one piece of 8" by 2" of the glossy paper and the green colored paper. Glue them together.

20. Apply glue on the top left corner of the strip. Slowly roll the paper into a long

cylinder, starting from the top left corner. Apply glue as you roll to secure the stem.

21. Attach the stem to the flower using ordinary glue or hot glue.

22. Cut 6" by 1" strip of green paper. Roll it below the petals and move downwards to cover the connection of the flower and the stem.

23. For this flower, the petal is essential. To make this, here are the steps:

    a. Cut 2 pieces of 1" x 6" of green paper with this pattern:

b. Glue a thin stick 1" from the top up to around the ¾ mark of the pattern of one of the pattern.

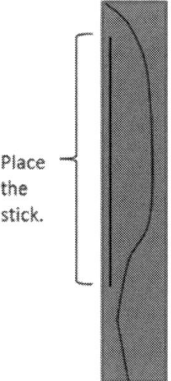

c. Apply glue on the edge of the leaf where the stick is placed. Place the other half on top of the stick to hide it.

d. Trim the top edge to make the leaf pointy. Glue the bottom of the two papers.

e. Attach the bottom of the leaf, to the stem.

f. If you have a transparent or green paper tape. You can wrap the tape around it to secure the leaf. Your flower would appear similar to this:

Marigold

Materials:

- 24" by 4" yellow crepe paper
- Green colored paper from the sepal and leaves
- Stick
- Glue

Directions:

1. Fold the yellow crepe paper in half, horizontally.

2. Draw a horizontal outline ½ inch from the bottom edge.

3. Cut equally wide vertical frills above the outline.

4. Carefully unfold the paper. Connect the edges again, but towards the other side. The frills would now be open. Glue the edges.

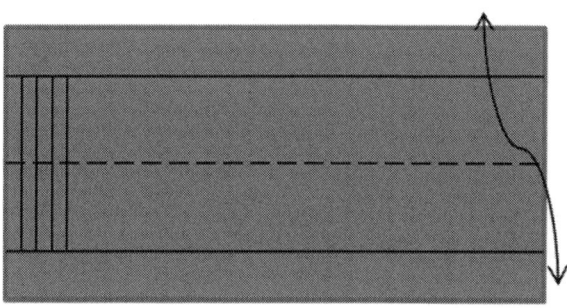

5. Get your stick. You do not have to cover it with green paper. Apply glue on one end of the paper and glue it to the stick. Roll the strip around the stick. Apply glue as you roll.

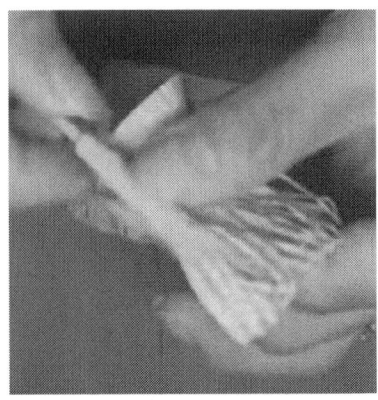

6. Take the green strip of paper and wrap the bottom of the flower. Continue to roll downward until you fully wrap the stem.

7. You can add leaves, if you like.

Sunflower

Materials:

- 1 piece 18" by ¾" black crepe paper
- 1 piece 18" by 1" brown crepe paper
- 1 piece 18" by 2" yellow crepe paper
- 1 piece 18" by 2.5" yellow crepe paper
- 1 piece 5" by 1" green crepe paper.

Directions:

1. Prepare the stigma by doing the following steps:

    a. Cut short vertical frills, about ¼ inch from the top edge of the black paper.

b. Roll the black strip from one end to the other.

c. Fold the brown crepe paper horizontally in half.

d. Cut frill on the top half of the paper.

e. Add it to the layer of the black strip.

2. Fold the smaller width yellow paper until the length is around ¾ inch.

3. Draw the following outline on the paper and cut it:

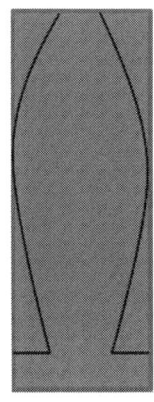

4. Fold the other yellow paper until the length is 1". Draw the same outline as the one above and cut.

5. Unfold the leaves and slightly curl the edges towards the middle.

6. Roll the smaller petals to the stigma until the end.

7. Continue with the larger petals.

8. For the sepal, fold the 5" by 1" green crepe paper in half twice, vertically. Draw the following pattern and cut:

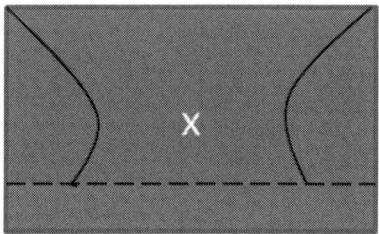

9. Wrap the sepal at the bottom part of the flower:

Note: If you want to add a stem, it would be better to add it in the beginning. Attach the tip of the stick to the black crepe paper before you begin rolling the center of the stigma.

Delphiniums

This is the easy method. If you want your delphiniums to look more detailed, you can check the sample discussed in Chapter 6.

Materials:

- 1 piece 8"x 3" paper of any color
- 1 piece 6"x 4" green paper
- 1 piece 5" x 3" green paper

``Direction:

1. Make a horizontal outline at the bottom of the 8" by 3" paper. Cut the top portion of the paper into ¼ inch" vertical fringes.
2. Curl each fringe by rolling the tip towards the edge of the fringe. Set aside.

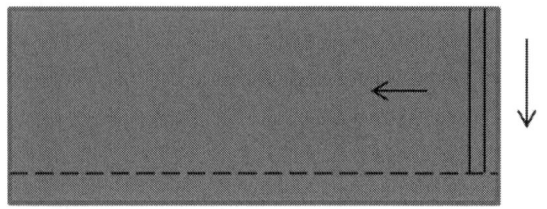

3. Take the 6" by 4" green paper. Roll it diagonally to make a long stick.
4. Take the petal strip. Make sure that the curls are directed to the outside. Wrap the tip of the stick twice. Then move the petals downward.
5. Make a ½ inch accordion style folds to the 5" by "3 green paper. Draw a ¼ inch outline at the bottom. Make an isosceles triangle at the top portion. Trace the outlines.

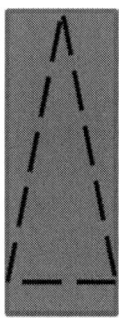

6. Unfold the leaves. Wrap the strip at the bottom of the petals.

Chapter 5 – Integrated Paper Flowers

The instructions in this chapter are for paper flowers which have petals that need to be separately created. The petals are glued together after to form the petals.

This type of paper flowers is a bit more detailed than the others. This is because some petals may have a different shape and size than the first layer. The stigma or the center of the flower is also a very important detail so do pay attention to it during the process.

Carnation

Materials:

- 5 pieces 8 x 8 onion-skin thin paper or tissue paper
- Stapler
- Scissors
- 1 1" by 1" thick paper, same color as the onion skin or green color

Directions:

1. Fold the papers in half, vertically and horizontally. Cut the paper into 4"-inch squares.

2. Stack the 20 squares and staple at the center.

3. Get a compass or any circle that could fit inside the square. Trace the circumference.

4. Trace the outline.

5. Take the top sheet and gather towards the center. Crumple the paper.

6. Gather the second sheet and crumple again.

7. Continue to with the other sheets.

8. Cut the 1-inch square into a circle and paste at the bottom of the flower.

9. If you want to add a stem to your carnation, roll a green strip of paper into a strong stick and attach it to the bottom of the flower.

Hibiscus

Materials:

- 5 pieces 2.5" x 3" crepe paper
- 1 piece 3" x ½" yellow paper
- 1 piece 7" x ½ crepe paper, same color as the 5 pieces
- 1 piece 2" x 4" green paper

Directions:

1. Prepare the center.

    a. Paste the 3" x ½" paper. To the 7" x ½" paper. Leave a 1 inch allowance from the tip of the 7" x ½".

    b. Fold them in half. Cut vertical fringes on the other half of the yellow part. Cut about 6 ½-inch horizontal fringes on the 1-inch allowance.

c. Flip the paper so the yellow part is at the bottom.

d. Start rolling the paper from the upper right corner, diagonally, until you have a soft stick.

e. Set aside.

2. Stack the 5 wide crepe papers together. Draw a pattern similar to the one below and cut.

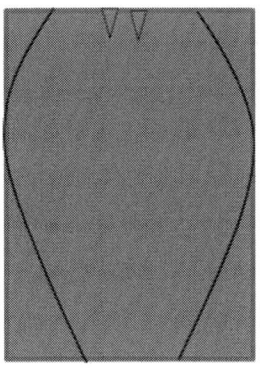

3. Assemble the petals.

a. Apply a thin strip of glue on the right lower portion of the petal.

b. Attach one petal. Repeat steps until you attach all the petals together.

c. Apply a thin strip of glue on the last petal and connect it with the left side of the first petal.

d. Crease the flowers lightly on the gaps.

4. Apply glue to the bottom part of the pistil, about ½ inch from the end.

5. Insert the pistil to the center of the flower.

6. Carefully pressed the bottom of the flower to the pistil. Ruffle the petals neatly.

7. Wrap the bottom with the green paper. Twist the ends of the green paper to form a soft stem.

Calla Lily

Materials:

- 1 piece of 4" x 3" paper, white, purple or pink
- 1 piece of 4" x 6" green paper
- 1 piece of 3" by ¾" yellow paper

Directions:

1. Roll the green paper diagonally, from one corner, until you create a strong stick.

2. Get the yellow paper and trace the following outline and cut

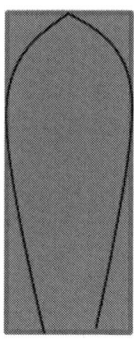

3. Roll and glue 1 inch of the bottom of the pistil to the stick.

4. Get the bigger paper. Trace and cut the following pattern:

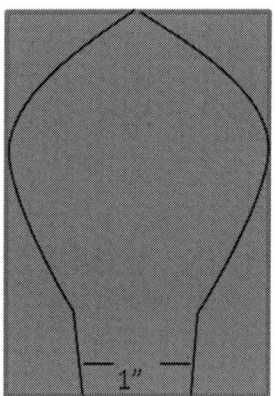

5. Wrap the petal around the stick and the pistil. Make sure that the opening of the pistil faces the petal.

6. Overlap the right edge of the petal to the left edge by about ½ inch. Glue only the bottom part, but the whole section

7. Add some leaf if you want. You can use the steps on making the daffodil leaf.

Roses

Materials:

- 4 pieces 4" x 4" colored paper, any color
- 1 piece 4" x 4" green colored paper

Directions:

1. Get 1 of the 4 colored papers. Fold it diagonally to get a triangle. Fold the triangle in half. Then, fold the smaller triangle in half, too.

2. Trace the following pattern to the small triangle and cut. You will end with an 8-petal 2D kirigami flower. Do the same to the other sheets of paper including the green paper.

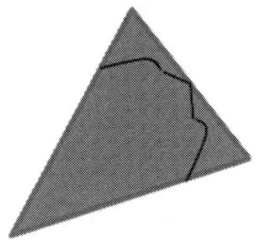

3. Cut one petal from the first sheet. Set aside. On the second and third sheet, cut 2-petals strip. Cut 3-petal strip from the last sheet.

4. Take a toothpick or any thin stick. Roll the tip of the petals outwards, slightly.

5. Take the one petal and roll it into a bud. Secure it with glue.

6. Take the 2-petal strip cut from the second sheet. Roll it into a bud, slightly bigger than the first bud. Secure with glue and set aside.

7. Take the other 2-petal strip from the third sheet. Apply glue on the edge of the right petal and connect the left edge of the left petal. Set aside.

8. Take the 3-petal strip Apply glue on the back side of the last petal. Attach the front side of the first petal. Set aside.

9. Take the 5-petal strip. Put some glue on the right edge of the last petal and connect it with the left edge of the first petal. Set aside.

10. Take the first 6-petal strip. Apply glue on the back of the last petal and paste the face of the first petal. Set aside.

11. For the last 6-petal strip, repeat step 8.

12. Assemble the petals.

    a. Take the last 6-petal layer. Put some glue on the inside bottom part of the petal. Insert the other 6-petal layer and glue the two layers together.

    b. Add the glue at the inside bottom part a the second layer and add the 5-petal layer.

    c. Continue to layer the petals until you end with the bud.

13. Take the green kirigami flower. Lower the cuts of the petal, so it will resemble as

leaves. Curl the leaves outward, so the tip points downward.

14. Place glue at the center of the green flower. Apply glue around the bottom of the rose.

15. Put the rose at the center of the green paper. Gather the green paper towards the rose.

16. Press the bottom part of the flower to secure the sepal.

17. If you want to add a stem, cut the point of the flower and insert a paper or wooden stick. Secure with green flower tape and cover the stem with green paper.

Anthurium

Materials:

- 1 piece 5" x 5" red or white crepe paper
- 1 piece 10" x ½" yellow crepe paper
- Green crepe paper
- 1 piece 2" x ½" crepe paper, same color as the 5" x 5"
- 1 piece 12" medium thick wire
- 1 piece tissue paper

Directions:

1. Fold the 5" x 5" paper into half, horizontally, to make a crease.

2. Using the crease as the guide, fold the paper thinly and in accordion style. Just like when you do the paper fan flower in chapter three.

3. Fold the gathered paper in half to make one half of the paper fan flower.

4. Take the 2" x ½" crepe paper and cut it into an isosceles triangle.

5. Make a crease on the triangle, about ½" from the base. Glue the crease of the triangle to the bottom of the paper fan.

6. Stretch the bottom of the paper fan until the top of the triangle is at the center of the paper fan. Secure it with glue.

7. Stretch the crepe paper to make the top part slightly flat.

8. Cut and shape the paper into an inverted heart.

9. Using the blunt side of your scissor, curl the edge of the flower towards you.

10. Get the tissue paper and fold it horizontally four times.

11. Apply glue on the tip of the wire and paste one end of the tissue paper. Roll the tissue paper spirally until you cover 2" of the wire.

12. Get the yellow paper and cover the layer of tissue.

13. Cover the rest of the wire with green paper.

14. Apply glue to the ½" inch tail of the heart and stick it to the bottom of the pistil.

15. Apply glue around the bottom of the pistil and attach sides of the opening of the heart.

Tulip

Materials:

- 5 pieces 5"x 2" crepe paper, any color of choice
- Green paper tape
- Green crepe paper
- Strong drinking straw
- 2 Long stick

Directions:

1. Fold the paper vertically in half.

2. Gather the bottom end of the folded paper. Stretch the upper part to form a scallop.

Do the same with the other four crepe papers.

3. Take one of the petals. Apply glue on the right edge, but only about ½ inch from the bottom of the petal. Place another petal on top. Do the same until you've attached all the petals.

4. Pinch the bottom of the petals together. Twist it tightly until it can fit into the hole of the drinking straw.

5. Insert the bottom of the paper in the drinking straw. Secure with green paper tape.

6. Insert a long stick at the other end of the drinking straw to support the stem. (Optional)

7. Cover the straw with a layer of green crepe paper.

8. To make the leaves, you can refer to the instruction in making the leaves of Narcissus or Daffodil in Chapter 4.

Anemone

Materials:

- 4 pieces 2" by 1" crepe paper, any color of choice for the petals
- 8 pieces 2" by 1.5" crepe paper, same color as the one above
- 2 piece 1.25" by 12" crepe paper, a darker shade than the petals
- Strong stick
- Green crepe paper
- Flexible thin wire

Directions:

1. Cut the petals in the following shape and set aside:

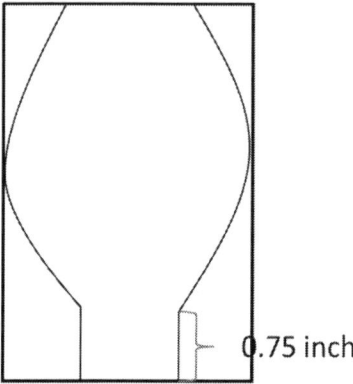

2. Take one of the 1.25" by 1" papers and roll it from one end to the other.

3. Fold the other 1.25" by 1" paper horizontally to make a crease. Cut the top part into thin strips, just like when you make the petals of the daisy in Chapter 4.

4. Twist the fringes to make it sturdy. Attach one end of the frilled paper to the rolled stigma and roll until the end.

5. Take the 2" by 1" petals. Stretch the crepe paper to make the petal form a scallop shape.

6. Attach the petals to the stigma on a perpendicular position.

7. Stretch the 2" by 1.5" petals, too. Arrange the petals around the pistil.

8. Roll a green paper at the bottom of the flower to serve as a sepal.

9. If you want the flower to have a stem, roll the stigma on a stick covered with green crepe paper.

Iris Flower

Materials:

- 8 pieces 2.5" by 1.5" white crepe paper
- 6 pieces 3" by 2" dark purple crepe paper
- 6 Pieces 3.25" by 2.25" light purple crepe paper
- 1 strong drinking straw.
- Green crepe paper
- 1 wooden stick

Directions:

1. Take the white crepe paper and cut it in this pattern:

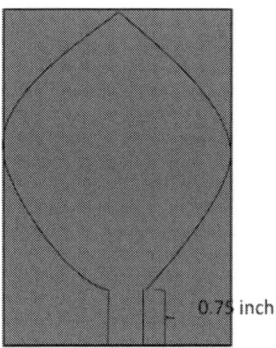

2. Take 2 of the white petals. Fold the petals vertically to make a light crease.

3. Apply glue on the middle portion of one of the petals. Place another petal on top of it. Stretch the petals vertically. Do the same to the other white papers. You will have 4 white petals.

4. Gather the petals together and arrange them in a perpendicular position. Secure the bottom with the flexible wire.

5. Pull the top part of the petals together. Keep them fix by applying glue. Set aside.

6. Take the lighter and darker crepe paper. Stack them together. The lighter paper should be at the bottom. Arrange carefully, so there would be a light edging on the inner side of the petal.

7. Cut the paper on this pattern:

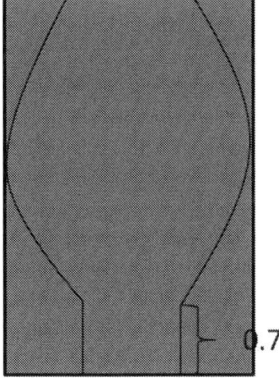

8. Stretch the papers horizontally to make a scallop shape.

9. Arrange and glue the petals to the white petals. Twist the ends to fit the hole of the drinking straw.

10. Insert the end of the flower to the drinking straw. Secure with green tape.

11. Insert a stick to the drinking straw to add support. (Optional)

12. Wrap the straw with green paper.

13. If you want to add leaves, use the instruction in making leaves for the Narcissus in Chapter 4.

Poppy Flower

Materials:

- 2 pieces 5" by 3" crepe paper, of any color
- 1 piece tissue paper
- 1 piece 0.75" by 7" black crepe paper
- 1 piece ¼" by 7" yellow crepe paper
- 1 piece 1" by 4" yellow crepe paper
- Green paper tape
- Stick

Directions:

1. Take the stick. Fold the tissue paper four times. Roll the paper on the stick to form a small ball. About ½ inch in size.

2. Wrap the ball with 1" by 4" yellow crepe paper.

3. Take the black and yellow strips. Glue the yellow strip on one edge of the black strip.

4. Fold the strip in half to form a crease.

5. Cut the yellow half of the strip into fringes. Twist the fringes to make round tips.

6. Wrap the fringed strip around the yellow ball.

7. Take one 5" by 3" crepe paper. Fold it in half. The opening part should be away from you.

8. Cut the paper in the following pattern:

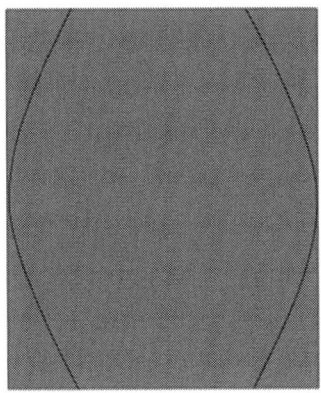

9. Cut a hole at the center of the paper. Do the same with the other paper.

10. Open the paper and insert the paper on the stick. Secure with glue.

11. Stretch the petals. Make creases on the edges of the petals. Use a pen or the blunt side of you scissors to curl the paper outward.

12. Insert the other set of petal on the stick. Arrange the petal, so they are perpendicularly positioned. Secure with glue.

13. Stretch the bottom petals. Make the same creases on the edges and curl the paper towards the inside.

14. Glue the edges of the petals together to make the petals pop.

15. Wrap the bottom of the flower and the stick with green paper.

16. To make the petal, cut a pattern similar to the petals, but use green paper.

17. Cut a small hole at the center and position it a few inches away from the paper. Press the bottom of the leaves. Secure with glue and green flower tape.

18. Wrap another layer of green crepe paper from the leaves down to the edge of the stick.

Birds of Paradise

Materials:

- 4 pieces of 4 ½" by 1 ½" orange crepe paper
- 2 pieces 4 ½" by 1" orange crepe paper
- 2 pieces 4 ½" by 1" purple or blue crepe paper
- 2 pieces 2" by ¾" purple or blue crepe paper
- 1 piece 2" by 6" green paper
- 1 piece 2" by 6" black paper
- Pink crayon

- Tissue paper
- Cotton
- Strip of white paper
- Thin wire
- 8" long thick wire

Directions:

1. Fold the 4 ½" papers vertically. Draw the pattern below and cut it:

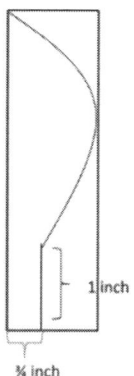

2. Fold the 2" by ¾" into half and draw the same pattern. However the paper would have this shape:

¾ inch

3. Cut a strip of ¼" by 5" of white crepe paper. Apply glue on the top surface and twist the paper to make a thin stick.

4. Get the purple or blue petal. Place a strip of glue on the crease.

5. Place the stick in the center and let it dry. Cut the excess stick. Do the same to the other purple flower.

6. Get 1 of the thinner orange petal. Apply a thin strip of glue on the crease and fold. Do not spread the glue. Only the middle portion should be glued. Do the same to the other orange petal

7. Get 2 of the wider orang petals and the small purple petal. Stack them together with the purple petal on top.

8. Place the bigger purple petal on top of the small purple petal. The step should be facing the orange petal.

9. Get the other orange paper. Open it and stack it above the large purple petal.

10. Tie the ends with the thin wire. Spread the petals and curl one of the largest orange petals outward. Make two sets of petals

11. Take the 2 pieces of 2" by 6" papers. Fold them horizontally.

12. Draw the same pattern as the petals on them, but do it a horizontal position.

13. Cut and paste the two leaves together.

14. Flip the leaf to show the black surface. Color the bottom and edges of the black leaf with the pink crayon.

15. Fold the leaf again horizontally. Make sure that the black part is on the outside. Set aside.

16. Get the thick wire and measure 3 inches from the top.

17. Using the pliers, bend the 3 inches to the side, slightly less than 90 degrees angle.

18. Take one of the flowers and place it just above the bended area. Securely tie the thin wire to the thick wire. Make sure that the 2 larger orange petals are on the left side.

19. Get the other flower and place it next to the first flower. Secure the thin wire with regular glue or hot glue.

20. Get the tissue paper and fold it into a long strip.

21. Apply glue on the stem. Roll the tissue paper from the bottom of the first flower down to the end of the wire.

22. Add glue to the angled stem. Place a layer of cotton around it, just enough so that the leaf can still cover it.

23. Glue the leaf on the angled stem. Make sure that the stem of the leaf is attached from the bended part. Apply glue on the cotton so it will hold the leaf on a convex

shape. No cotton should be visible from the sides.

24. Use a green tape or extra green crepe paper to cover the unhidden portions of the tissue paper. Continue to cover it until the stem is thick enough.

25. Add more leaves if you desire. Just follow the instructions on making the green-black leaf and attach them on the longer side of the stem.

Chapter 6 – Cluster Flowers

In this chapter, the flowers are much smaller in size as they will be bundled together. They are easy to make, but you need to have a lot of patience. This is especially so if you want to add more realistic details to the flowers you're creating.

If you are planning to create bouquet of flowers, wreath or flower crowns, these flowers can be great for those projects.

Lily in the Valley

Materials:

- 7 pieces 2" x 2"
- Medium thick flexible tape
- 1 strong drinking straw
- Green crepe papers
- Thin sticks for the leaves
- 1 stick for support (optional)

Directions:

1. Take a white paper. Fold it horizontally with the open part away from you. Cut this pattern.

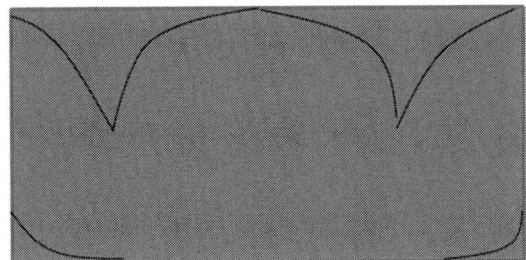

2. Open the paper and connect the ends the two end petals to form four petals. See the figure below:

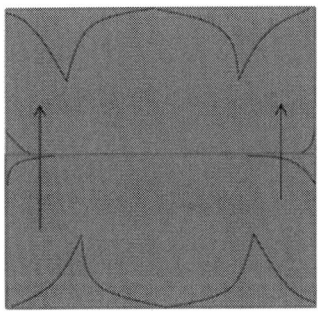

3. Cut a 2" of the flexible wire. Wrap it with green crepe paper.

4. Inset the petal on the wire by making a hole at the center of the flower. Secure

with glue. Set aside. Make 6 flowers or more if you desire.

5. Get the drinking straw and wrap it with green paper. Insert a stick on the straw if it needs more support.

6. Attach the flowers to the stick using the green flower tape. Reinforced with a few layers of the green paper.

7. To cover the tip of the straw, make a bud. You can do this by attaching the petal tips of one of the flowers.

8. Insert the wire on the opening of the straw and secure with tape. Cover with another layer of green paper.

9. Make 4 leaves similar to the leaves of the Narcissus in Chapter 4. Arrange it around the stem to complete the look.

Wisteria

This type of flower is often used to decorate the popular attractions known as flower tunnels in Japan. It is easy to make, but it can take you longer because you have to make it in clusters. Wisteria often grows 24 flowers on one stalk. But, ½ of the stalk is often filled with wisteria buds.

Materials:

- 2 shades of crepe papers, but Japanese papers are more preferred, pink or violet
- Green crepe paper or Japanese paper
- Thick flexible wire
- Thin flexible wire
- Green flower tape

Directions:

1. Prepare the buds. To do this, cut 20 pieces of 1"x ½" of the paper. You will have a set for each shade.

2. Cut the paper into oblong shape. Make sure that you cut them uniformly.

3. Make 20 stems by cutting the thin wire into 2-inch long sticks. Cover the wire with green crepe paper.

4. Get a darker shade oblong. Apply glue all over it. Place the wire at the center. Top with a lighter shade oblong. Make 20 pieces of these buds, set aside.

5. Make flowers. The wisteria usually only have two petals and it is joined with another bud at the center. So, to do this, cut 20 pieces of 1" x 1" of the paper, but use only a paper with lighter shade.

6. Cut this pattern on the paper:

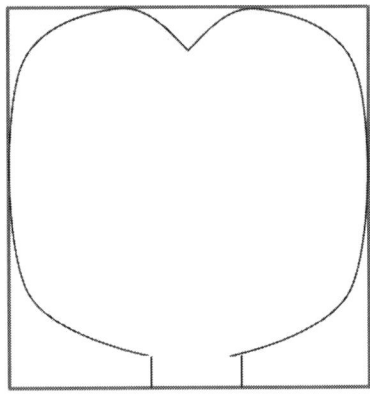

7. Curl the petal outward using the blunt side of your scissor or a pen.

8. Get one bud. Glue the bottom of two leaves on the wire. Make sure that the petals are close to each other.

9. Secure the petals with flower tape and reinforce with crepe paper. Do ten of the flower set.

To assemble the flower:

1. Cut an 8" long thick wire. Wrap it with green paper

2. Take the ten buds and arrange them on the top part of the wire. To attach them, simply wrap the wire on the stem. Reinforce with tape and crepe paper.

3. When you reach the middle part of the stick, attach the flowers in the same manner. Arrange them so they would look like a cluster.

4. Since Wisteria is a vine flower, you may have to make the leaves differently. Here how:

    a. Cut 1 piece 12" long thick wire. Wrap it with green paper.

    b. Cut 8 to 10 pieces of 2" by 1.5" strips of green crepe papers.

    c. Shape them into regular leaves.

    d. Cut 3" strips of the thin wire and wrap it with crepe papers.

    e. Place a wire under the leaves. Secure it with glue. Twist it on the thick wire. Arrange the leaves on the stick.

    f. Attach the flower cluster at the center of the row of leaves.

Apricot Flowers

Materials:

- 1 piece 1" x 1" green paper.
- 7 pieces 1" by ½" yellow crepe paper
- 1 piece ¾" by 2" yellow crepe paper
- 1 piece ¼" by 2" orange or red crepe paper
- Thin wire
- 1 piece 6" thick wire, optional
- Green flower tape
- Yellow flower tape
- Tissue paper
- Needle or anything that can punch a hole on a paper

Directions:

1. Make the stigma by doing the following:

    a. Cut a ½" x 1" tissue paper.

    b. Cut a 4" long thin wire.

    c. Wrap the tissue paper to one end of the wire. Form a ball. Wrap it with yellow. Cover at least 1/3 of the wire with the tape. Set aside.

    d. Pate the orange strip on the upper half of the yellow strip.

    e. Cut about 10 to 15 fringes on the paper. Make sure to leave an allowance of at least ¼" at the bottom.

    f. Twist the fringes so they will look rounded. Wrap them around the yellow ball. Set aside

2. Prepare the petals:

    a. Fold the 1" x 1" green paper into four parts and cut this pattern:

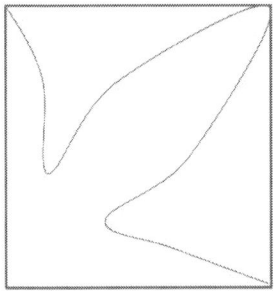

b. Punch a small hole at the center of the sepal.

c. Fold the 1" x ½" papers vertically and cut this pattern.

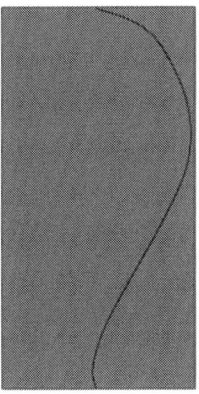

d. Open the paper and stretch the petals.

e. Arrange the petals on the green paper. Make sure not to cover the small hole.

3. Get the stigma and insert the wire through the hole. Settle the stigma at the center and secure with clear glue.

4. Wrap the rest of the wire with green tape or crepe paper.

5. Make some leaves by cutting 2 1" x 1.5" inch rectangle using green paper. Shape and cut 2 regular leafs.

6. Cut 2 pieces of 2" long thin wire. Wrap it with green paper. Glue it at the back of a leaf.

7. Attach it on the stem of the apricot flower. Make 5 or more of the flowers Set aside

8. Wrap the thick wire or stick with green crepe paper.

9. Arrange the flower on the thick wire. Attach it by twisting the ends of the stem on the twig. Secure with green tape or reinforce with another layer of crepe paper.

Baby's breath

This tiny flower always adds a touch of rustic sophistication to a bouquet of flowers. Making a cluster of this can be challenging in terms of time, but it is easy and the steps are similar to the apricot flower. However, the petals would be smaller and you have to create more flowers to create a cluster.

Materials:

- About 40 of ½" by ½", white, pink or lavender paper
- Green paper
- Thin wire
- Yellow or light brown tape
- Yellow beads
- Needle

- Medium thick wire 6" long, optional

Directions:

1. Make a kirigami petal.

    a. Fold the paper diagonally to make a triangle. Then, fold the triangle twice, so you will have an 8-petal flower.

    b. Cut the paper into the following pattern:

    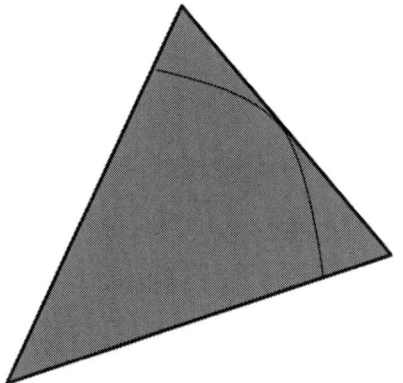

    c. Open the petals.

    d. Get the green paper and punch little circles from it. You can use a puncher for this.

e. Place a circle green paper at the center of the petal. This shall serve as the sepal. Flip the petal.

f. Cut 2" long thin wire. Wrap the end with the yellow tape, just enough so the bead would not slip out.

g. Insert a bead on the wire.

h. Punch a small hole at the center of the petal. Insert the wire until the bead is settled at the center. Secure with glue.

i. Wrap the wire with green paper or tape. Set aside.

j. Make 40 of these flowers and cluster them by 5 flowers or more.

k. Wrap the thick wire or the stick with green paper and attach the cluster of flowers.

Delphiniums

Materials:

- 4 pieces 1" by 1" white crepe paper
- 4 pieces 1" by 1" crepe paper, any color
- 6 pieces 1.5" by 1.5" crepe paper, similar to the 1" x 1" or a darker shade
- 1 piece ½" x 1.5" black paper, or a shade darker than the petals
- thin wires
- Green tape
- Green paper
- 1 6-inch long, thick flexible wire

Directions:

1. Cut a 2" long thin wire. Wrap the tip using the black paper.

2. Get one piece of the 1" by 1" white paper. Fold it equally and in accordion way three times. Make sure that the 4 parts are equal.

3. Cut the following pattern and do the same to the other white papers:

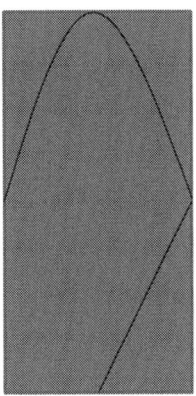

4. Arrange the petals around the center in a perpendicular way.

5. Get the 1" by 1" colored papers, cut them in the following pattern:

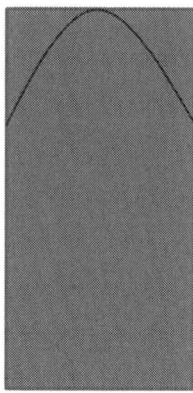

6. Make a small crease at the bottom middle of the petal. Gather the ends of the petal and paste it the crease. Do the same to all the second layer petals.

7. Arrange the petals around the first layer.

8. Repeat the steps of making the second layer petals to the 1.5" by 1.5" papers.

9. Attach the petals after the second layer.

10. Wrap the bottom of the flower with green tape and cover it with a layer of green paper.

11. Make about 12 to 15 of these flowers and set aside.

12. Wrap the flexible wire with green paper. Place one flower on top of the stick. Secure it by twisting the wire and by reinforcing it with glue or green tape.

13. Arrange the other flowers at the bottom.

14. Make the same leaves as discussed in Chapter 4. Wrap the strip around the remaining part of the wire.

Bells of Ireland

Many people debate whether the bells of Ireland are flowers or leaves because of its green color. But, it is really a flower and can be a good addition to some bouquets or table center decorations.

Materials:

- 24 pieces of ½" by 1" green paper
- 20 pieces of 1" by 1 ½" green paper
- 16 pieces 1" by 2" green paper
- 5 strips of ½" by 12" pink or white paper crepe paper
- Extra green paper
- Tissue
- 1 piece 8" long thick wire
- Tissue paper
- Thin wire

Directions:

1. Stack the papers of different sizes and uniformly cut them in this shape:

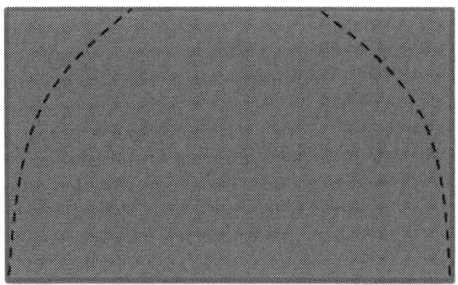

2. Cut 60 pieces of 2 ½" long thin wires. Wrap one tip of the wires with 3 round of pink or white crepe paper. Wrap the rest of the wire with green tape or green crepe paper.

3. Take 1 of the green petals. Fold the bottom-middle part to make a crease.

4. Apply a strip of glue at the end crease. Place the stigma in the center. Make sure that the end of pink tip is parallel to the bottom of the petal.

5. Make a cone out of the semi-circle by placing the back side of the right edge to the top side of the left edge. Do this to all the petals.

6. Bend the thick wire a little, just to have a little curve. Thicken the strong wire with a long strip of tissue paper.

7. Wrap the stem with one layer of green crepe paper or green tape.

8. Get the smallest bell flowers and arrange them at the top part of the stick. Tie them securely to the thick wire.

9. Place the medium bell flowers in the middle. Do not add them so close to each other.

10. Add the big bell flowers at the bottom. Arrange them so that the more of the stem may also be viewed.

Gladiolus

Materials:

- 6 pieces 1" by 4" yellow paper or any color desired
- 6 pieces 1 ½" by 8" yellow paper or any color desired
- 12 pieces 1" by 1 ½" green paper
- 6 pieces of 2" by 3" green paper
- 6 pieces ½" by 1 ½" green paper
- 1 piece 8-inch thick stick
- 12 pieces 2-inch thin wires
- 12 pieces 1" by 1" pink paper
- Green tape and extra green crepe paper
- Tissue paper

Directions:

1. Get the thick wire and thicken it using a tissue paper. Cover it with green crepe paper and set aside.

2. Stack all the 1" by 1" pink paper. Draw and cut the following pattern:

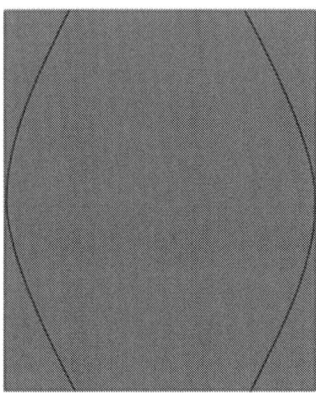

3. Make a crease at the bottom-middle part of the pink petal. Gather the bottom part towards the crease and press it tightly. Do this to another petal.

4. Glue the bottom of the two petals together. You will end up with a two-petal tulip bud. Set aside.

5. Get the 8" strip of yellow crepe paper. Fold it in accordion style until you have 8 rectangles.

6. Draw and cut the following pattern:

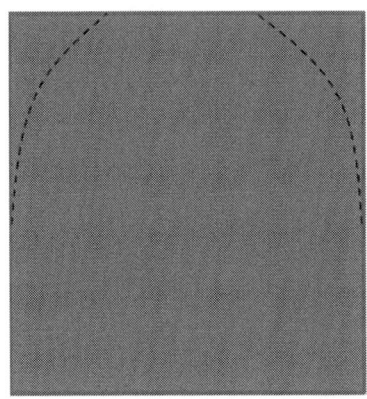

7. Curl the tip of the petals outward. Add them to the first layer of pink petal. You should have 2 layers of yellow petal. Secure the bottom with thin wire. Make 6 of this flower.

8. Get the 4" yellow strip. Fold them in accordion style until you get 8 rectangles.

9. Draw and cut the same pattern above.

10. Curl the petals and roll into a half-bloomed buds. You should have at least three layers of petals for each bud.

11. Tie the bottom with thin wire to secure the flower. Make a total of six of this flower. Set aside.

12. Get the 1 ½" by 1" green paper. Stuck them together and cut them in the following pattern:

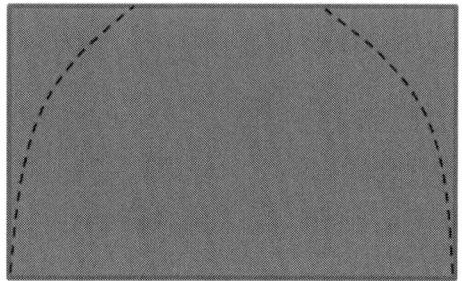

13. Twist the green paper to make a cone. Secure the shape with glue.

14. Place a yellow bud on top of the green sepal. Tie the bottom with the thin wire attached to the bud.

15. Cover the bottom and the wire with green crepe paper or green tape.

16. Do the same with the large flowers. However, with the large flowers, the bottom of the flower may only be halfway of the cone. Cut the excess tip, but do not cut the wire from the flower.

17. Secure the bottom of the flower with the wire. Reinforce with green paper or green tape.

18. Get the ½" by 1 ½ green paper and fold it horizontally. Draw and cut the following pattern on the paper:

19. Do the same with the 2" by 3" green paper.

20. Get the smaller leaves. Add a tiny strip of glue on the crease, except on the step part. Fold and glue the center. Let it dry for a while. Do the same to the larger leaves.

To assemble:

1. Get the prepared stem.

2. Arrange the 6 small leaves on the tip of the stem.

3. Follow it up with the 6 buds. Tie the buds using the thin wire. Wrap another layer of green paper or green tape around each tied spot.

4. Place 2 large leaf after the buds.

5. Arrange the 6 large flowers on the next portion of the stem. Hide the wires using the green tape or green papers again.

6. Add the remaining leaves after the large flowers.

Chapter 7: Flower Buds

In some flower arrangements, flower buds are essential. They add shape and variety. Creating flower buds can be easy, but it can also be a little tricky. Here are different methods when it comes to creating flowers buds you can use together with your flower clusters.

Carnation, Hibiscus and Poppy Buds

Materials:

- 4 pieces 2" by ½" Crepe Paper of any choice
- 1 piece 2" by 4" green crepe paper
- Thin stick
- Extra green crepe paper
- Tissue paper

Directions:

1. Cut a strip from a tissue paper, about 2" width.

2. Roll the tissue paper to the stick. Make a 2" corndog shape on one end of the stick.

3. Take the 2 by ½" crepe paper and cut it into this pattern:

4. Stretch the petals and cover the tissue paper.

5. Get the 2" x 4" strip green paper and fold it into 8. Cut the following pattern:

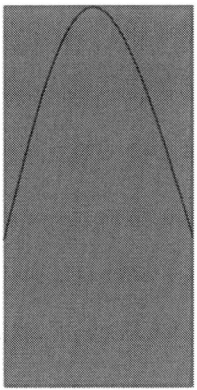

6. Wrap the buds with the green strip. Make sure that the point of the sepal is about ¼" away from the tip of the bud.

7. Cut a long strip of green paper. Wrap it at the bottom of the bud to pull the ends of the sepal to the stick. Continue to wrap until you cover all the stick.

8. Add thin ordinary-shaped leaves on the stems if you want.

Note: This is also the same steps in making the Hibiscus and Poppy bud except for the following difference:

1. The bud size is about ½" inch longer.

2. The sepal is ½ inch shorter.

3. The leaves are wider.

Rose Buds

Materials:

- 2 pieces 4" x 4" colored paper, any color
- 1 piece 4" x 4" green colored paper
- Thick flexible stick
- Extra green crepe paper
- Tissue paper

Directions:

1. Take the 4" x 4" colored paper and fold it, diagonally. Fold it again into triangle twice.

2. Cut the following pattern to make the rose petal:

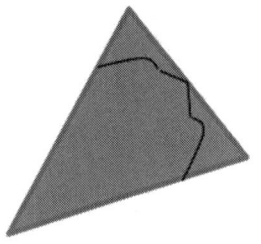

3. Cut 2 of the petal and set aside. You will have 2 strips made of 2 petals and 2 strips of 6 petals.

4. Cut a short strip of tissue paper. Attach one of the ends to the stick and roll into a ball. Make sure that the ball is about 1" in diameter.

5. Get the 2 strips of 2 petals and use it to cover the ball. The strips may not cover the whole ball, but do not worry. Glue the tip of the petals together.

6. Get one of the 6-petal strips and roll it on the first layer. Glue the tips of the petals together.

7. Take the other strip and add it as the last layer.

8. Roll the tips of the last layer outward using a toothpick or a thin stick.

9. For the sepal, cut the green paper like it was a petal, but shorten the petal by about ¼ inch.

10. Add the green paper as the last layer of the bud.

11. Secure the bottom with green paper tape and cover with another layer of green paper.

12. Add leaves if you want.

Tulip

Materials:

- 5 pieces 5"x 2" crepe paper, any color of choice
- Green paper tape
- Green crepe paper
- Strong drinking straw
- Tissue paper
- 1 stick

Directions:

1. Make a 1.5" by ½" corndog-shaped bud using the tissue paper and the stick. See the instruction on how to make the shape in steps 1 and 2 of making carnation buds.

2. Make 5 regular petals of the tulip. See the instruction in Chapter 5 on how to make the petal.

3. Get on of the petal. Roll it to the corndog bud. Add the other petal, but do not add it to the end of the first petal. Start at the center of the first petal. Repeat the steps until you rolled all the 5 petals.

4. Insert the stick to the straw.

5. Wrap a green tape at the bottom to secure the bud. Reinforce with green paper.

6. Cover the stem with green paper. Add the leaves, as discussed in chapter 5.

Note: If you want your bud to be close to blooming, turn the corndog into a ball with the size of 1.5" in diameter.

Calla Lily Buds

Materials:

- 1 piece 4" x 3" paper, white, purple or pink
- 1 piece of 3 by 3" green paper
- 1 completed stalk with pistil of Calla Lily (one without the petal)

Directions:

1. Make the center of the flower as instructed in Chapter 5.

2. Stack the 4" x 3" and 3" x 3" papers. Make sure that the green paper is at the bottom. Glue them together.

3. Trace and shape the paper into a petal of calla lily. You can find the pattern in Chapter 5.

4. Attach one end of the petal to the bottom of the stigma and roll it around until only the tip of the stigma can be seen.

5. Complete the look by finishing the bud, just as you would finish the bloomed flower.

Iris Flower and Narcissus Bud

There are two ways of making the buds for iris flowers. The first is the same as the tulip buds, but you will only add a layer of green petals, which are about 1/3" shorter than the petals. But, when you are making bouquets or wreaths, it would be better to use half-bloomed buds and this is how you could do it:

Materials:

- 4 pieces 3.5" by 1.5" white crepe paper
- 4 pieces 3" by 1.5" dark purple crepe paper
- 6 Pieces 3" by ½" Green crepe paper
- 1 strong drinking straw.
- Green crepe paper
- 1 wooden stick
- Tissue paper

Direction:

1. Make a 1.5" by ½ inch corndog-shape at one end of the stick by using the tissue paper.

2. Cut the white crepe paper in the following pattern:

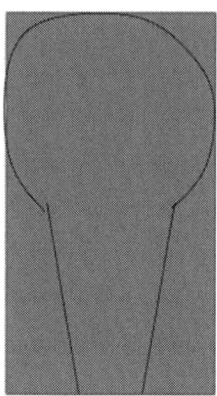

3. Use the blunt side of your scissor to curl the tip of the petal outward.

4. Wrap the petal to the corndog tip. Make sure that only a small part the curved part of the petal is glued to the tissue paper bud.

5. Cut the purple paper in the following pattern:

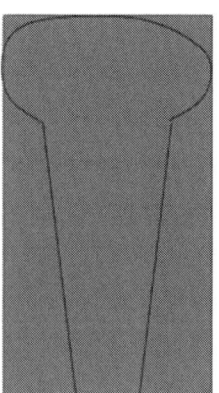

6. Arrange the purple petal in between the white petals. Do not curl the petal.

7. Get the green paper and cut in the following pattern:

8. Glue each green petal around the flower. Do not glue the tip.

9. Get a piece of toothpick and use it to curl the green petals alternately.

10. Insert the stick into a straw and finish the bud, just as you would finish the actual flower.

Note: The Narcissus bud will also have the same steps except for the following differences:

- The inner petals and the outside petals are of the same sizes.

- The petals are curved inside

- The sepal leaves are only half the height of the petals and they are glued all the way to the tip.

Daisy, Sunflower and Calendula Bud

The buds of these flowers can be an attractive addition to large bouquets and wreaths. Making them is almost the same as making a basic flower, but with a few tweaks on the measurements and petal curling.

Materials:

- Tissue paper
- Stick
- Black or brown crepe paper
- 2 piece 2" by 3" yellow paper
- 1 piece 1.5" by 3" green paper
- Extra green paper for stem and leaves

Directions:

1. Make a 1" ball at the tip of the stick.

2. Cover the ball with black crepe paper. If you are going to use brown paper, make black dots on the top of the ball using a black marking pen.

3. Take the 2" pieces of yellow paper. Make a horizontal crease at the middle and fringe the other half.

4. Take 1 piece of the fringe yellow paper and curl it inward. Make sure that the tips almost touch the crease line. Set aside.

5. Take the other piece and curl it slightly outward.

6. Wrap the first strip of yellow paper to the black ball. Arrange the fringes, so that the black ball is almost hidden.

7. Add the second layer of yellow paper.

8. Get the 1.5" by 3" green strip of green paper. Fringe the top ¼" portion of the strip.

9. Wrap it all over the bud.

10. Cut a long strip of green paper and wrap it around the bud twice and slowly move it down to cover the stick.

11. Add leaves if you desire.

Calendula bud

Materials:

Same as materials used for the previous style except for the sizes. All the strips for the calendula bud should have a uniform width of 1.5".

Directions:

1. Fringe all the yellow strips as instructed above. Curl one of the strips inward, but leave the second strip as it is.

2. After making the 1" black ball, wrap the curled fringed strip to the ball.

3. Add the second strip.

4. For the green strip, widen the fringe a little and make it point, just like this pattern.

5. Curl the pointy part of the fringes, slightly. Wrap it to the bud.

6. Secure the bottom of the bud with the extra green paper strip and finish the bud, just as you would finish the flower in Chapter 4.

Anemone

Materials:

- 5 pieces 2" by 1" crepe paper, any color of choice for the petals
- 5 pieces 2" by 1" green crepe paper
- Strong stick
- Green crepe paper

Directions:

1. Cut the 2" by 1" crepe papers in the same pattern as the petal. See the pattern below:

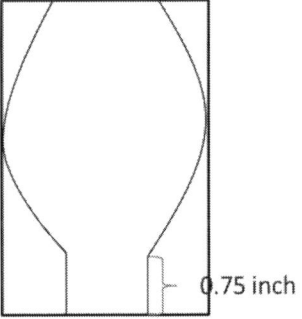

2. Take the green papers. Stack them together and cut 3 inverted small triangles on the tip of the petal.

3. Stack one colored petal and green paper together. The green paper should be at the bottom.

4. Take one petal and glue ¼" of its right edge to the ¼" of the left edge of another petal. Do this until you attached all the petals.

5. Roll the strip of petals. If you want a tight bud, roll it tightly. If you want a half-bloom petals, roll it lightly and curl the tips of the petal, slightly.

6. Secure the roll with glue.

7. Take a long strip of green paper and roll it at the bottom portion of the bud. Continue to roll it downward until you cover the stick or the wire.

Poppy Flower Buds

Poppy flowers typically have a hard-shell bud. The sepal that protects the bud is as strong as a nut. To make this particular hard-shell bud, here are the materials and the steps.

Materials:

- Tissue paper
- 6" long flexible thick wire
- 2 pieces 1" by 3" green crepe paper
- Extra green crepe paper
- Thread or thin flexible wire

Directions:

1. Wrap the tissue around the thick wire and make a 1" ball. Secure with glue.

2. Fold the 1" by 3" green crepe paper vertically in half. Twist a thread or thin wire the open edge together to close it. You will end up with something that is similar to the petal of the tulip, as discussed in Chapter 5.

3. Stretch the paper to make a scallop shape. Do the same to the other strip.

4. Place the two flowers and cover the ball like a nut.

5. Wrap the bottom with extra green paper and finish the stem.

Half-bloom Bud

- Tissue paper

- 6" long flexible thick wire

- 2 pieces 1" by 3" green crepe paper

- Extra green crepe paper

- Thread or thin flexible wire

Directions:

1. Make the Poppy flower as instructed in Chapter 5.

2. Stretch the sepal so it could cover a lot of the petals.

3. Roll the thread or the thin wire around the sepal to tighten the petals together.

4. Cover the tied portion with green paper and the rest of the stem.

5. Using a toothpick or a small round stick, curl the tip to outward.

Anthurium Bud

If you have your anthurium petal prepared, follow the steps below in order to create the bud using the pre-made flower.

Directions:

1. Cut about ¼ of the right side of the flower.

2. Carefully, roll the flower towards the sepal to cover it. Secure with glue.

3. Curl the left corner of the flower towards the right side until it rolls towards the rolled right side.

If you want a pure bud, cut the edges of the petal by about 1/3. Roll the right side to the center and then roll the left side so that t overlaps with the right side. You will have a shape similar to a chili pepper.

Peony Bud

A peony bud can look like a little colored cabbage. But, if you add a little curl on the outer petals and make it slightly bloom, you will have a nice addition to your peony or rose bouquet.

Materials:

- Tissue paper
- 1 strong stick
- 24 pieces 1.5" by 1" crepe paper, white, pink or red
- 4 pieces 1" by 2" green crepe paper
- Extra green crepe paper for the stem and flowers.

Directions:

1. Wrap the tissue around the tip of the stick until you form a 1" ball.

2. Cut the 24 pieces of crepe paper using this pattern:

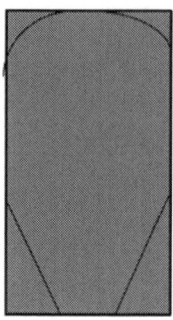

3. Reserve 8 pieces of the petals.

4. Cover the ball with the petals. The first layer should be glued all the way to the top of the ball. The next layers will leave about ¼" of the petal unglued.

5. Use the reserved 8 pieces for the last layer. Make 2 slits of about ¼" long on the tip of each of the petal. The tip will now have three parts.

6. Curl the two sides slightly, but leave the middle part as it is.

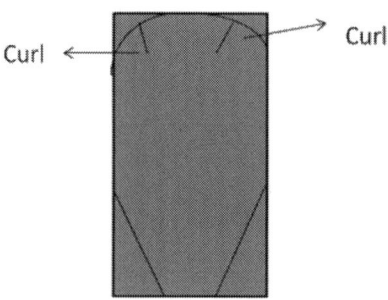

7. Glue the last layer of petal only halfway.

8. Take the 1" by 2" green crepe papers and fold them in half vertically. Form them just like the sepal of the Poppy flower.

9. Stretch and curl them outward. Arrange them around the bud.

10. Complete the stem by wrapping it with green paper and decorating it with leaves.

Chapter 8: Simple Projects Using Paper Flowers

Scented Flower Vase

Materials:

- Small glass vase or , about 4" tall and 2" wide
- Paper flowers (Lavender, Rose or peony and a 2 stalk of baby's breath)
- Essential oil
- Shallow bowl, about 4" or 6" in diameter
- Crystals or marbles
- Potpourris, light scented
- Hot glue
- Barbecue skewers, 8" long
- 3 pieces of ½" by 5" white paper
- 3 pieces of ½" by 5" paper that matches the color of your flowers.
- Green paper tape or extra green paper
- Green or silver dusts
- Blue coloring water

Directions:

1. Make a total of 4 paper flowers as instructed by the book. However, make the following changes:

a. Use bamboo skewers as the stem. Cut off the pointy tip.

b. Use only Japanese papers or crepe papers

c. Do not cover the top part of the tip of the stick when wrapping the stigma.

d. Only cover about 1" of the stem, from the bottom of the flower.

2. Get the 3" white strip. Pull the two ends together to make a bunny head. Twist the ends together to secure the shape.

3. Get the 3" strip of a different color. Make another bunny head.

4. Put two different bunny-head shapes on each side of the bamboo skewer. Attach with hot glue or by tape. Make 3 of this accessory.

5. Glue the base of the vase in the center of the bowl.

6. Pour a layer of potpourris on the bowl and top with a layer of crystals and marbles.

7. Pour about 3 ounces of blue colored water on the vase. Pour a pinch of silver dust.

8. Arrange the flowers you made inside the vase.

9. Put a few drops of essential oil on the stigma of the flower. Make sure to target the bamboo skewer. Put a few more drops on the potpourris.

10. Place on the table or anywhere where you want to be relaxed.

Flower Pomanders

If you are having a party in a small venue, adding these hanging flowers add more visual interest to the space without taking up more of the limited foot area.

Materials:

- Styrofoam ball of any size
- Tissue paper
- Wrapping paper, same color as the motif or any of the flower
- Skewer, bamboo or metal
- Paper flowers and buds (carnation, roses, daisy)
- Tissue paper
- Wide strips of crepe paper, preferably white or a color that is a lighter shade than the flowers

- 1 piece "J" or round hook
- 1 thick stick, about ½" thick in diameter and 3" long
- Hot glue
- Ribbon (optional)

Directions:

1. Attach the J-hook at the center of the ball using hot glue.

2. At the opposite of the J-hook, punch the thick stick. Leave at least 2" of the stick sticking out. Secure with hot glue again.

3. Brush the ball with regular glue or paste. Cover with one layer of tissue paper. Do not worry if the cover is not smooth.

4. For the second layer, cover the ball with the wrapping paper.

5. Cover the stick with the wrapping paper, too. At this point, you can now set aside the ball and proceed with making your flowers. Or, you can add the next design element.

6. Make 1" width long strips of the wrapping paper. Fringe ½ of the strip. Add a layer of fringed strips to the ball. Set aside

Note: You do not have to cover the whole ball with the fringed strips.

7. Make your paper flowers. You can opt for the following:

    a. Make the same size of flowers and buds regardless of the size of your ball; or

    b. Adjust the size of your flowers and buds.

    In making your flowers, use skewers for the stem. Make sure that the stem is at least 1" long.

8. Arrange the flowers on the ball. To do this, place hot glue at the bottom of the flower. Then, punch the stem into the ball. Cover the ball first with flowers.

9. For spaces, where flowers could not fit, you can place the buds.

10. Tie a paper ribbon on the stick to complete the look.

Flower-Bordered Picture Frame

Materials:

- 3 pieces 8" by 6" cardboard
- 2 pieces 5" by 3" cardboard
- 1 piece 6 ½" by 4 ½" clear hard plastic or thin glass
- Wrapping paper
- Strong glue or hot glue
- Flowers (1 big sunflower or daisy, about 2" in size and about 4 pieces of 1" size.
- Small stickers of flowers; or
- Neon glue

Directions:

1. Take two pieces of the 8" by 6"cardboard. Stack them together and cut a 6" by 4" rectangle on each of them. You can put it in the middle or slightly off to one side. The rectangle should be equal and in the same position for both cardboard. These boards will serve as the frames.

2. Get one of the frames. Wrap it with wrapping paper of your choice. Make sure that you keep the back side of the frame smooth.

3. Attach the glass on the frame. Use hot glue or any strong glue.

4. Take the other frame. Cut the top border of the frame. Do not extend to the left and right border.

5. Cover the second frame with wrapping paper.

6. Attach the second frame at the back of the first frame. Secure with strong glue.

7. Take the last 8" x 6" board. Make a T-line in the middle, about 4" high from the bottom edge. The horizontal line should be about 3".

8. Using a cutter or blade, cut a slit on the horizontal line. Set aside.

9. Stack the 2 pieces of 5" by 3" cardboard. Measure a ½" allowance from the top of one of the boards. Cut the allowance. Now, you will have a 5" x 3" cardboard and a 4 ½" x 3 cardboard.

10. Glue the two cardboards together. The shorter one should be under the longer one.

11. Wrap the cardboard with wrapping paper, but do not cover the hanging ½" of the other board.

12. Fold the ½" allowance backward to make a crease. Insert the hanging part into the slit in the 8" x 6" cardboard. Secure it with strong glue.

13. Wrap the last 8" x 6" cardboard.

14. Attach the first frame to the back frame. The base picture frame is finished.

15. Decorate the borders with paper flowers. Here are some points and suggestions:

a. Do not use stick or wire for the stem. Use rolled paper, instead. This way, you can cut through it.

b. Flatten the bottom of the flowers by cutting the pointy bottom.

c. Full bloom paper flowers are better to use, such as daisy, sunflower, and roses. You can also use cherry blossom, Kusuduma and paper fan flowers.

d. In placing the flowers, use only small flowers. However, you can put a big flower to draw the attention to a certain point. For example, if your face is somewhere in the middle, place the biggest flower near the middle to draw attention.

e. Put less flowers if there are many people or objects in the picture.

f. Do not overcrowd more than two spots. For example, you can place a bunch of flowers on all four corners. It will take away a lot from the picture.

Paper Flower Crowns

Materials:

- Paper rose flower, various sizes and colors, a few buds
- Rose leaves
- Strips of green paper
- Medium thick wire
- Thin wire
- Green tape
- ¼" ribbon, same color as the petal of the flower
- Tape measure

Directions:

1. Measure the size of your head from your forehead to around the back. For this project, we will follow the standard 18-inch crown.

2. Cut two 20-inches long medium thick wire. Wrap it with green paper.

3. Put the two stick together. Tie one of the ends together with thin wire. Cover with green tape.

4. Braid the two wires together. Tie the other end with another thin wire and cover with green tape.

5. Bend the braided wire to form a circle. You can tie the two ends together with wire or you can leave it open.

6. Cut 2" long thin wires. Tie some thin wire around the bottom of the flowers and buds. Leave about 1" tail. Cover the tied portion and the tail with green tape.

7. Arrange and tie the flowers on the wreath.

8. Make the leaves. To make them, paste a thin wire in the middle of one of the leaves.

Top it with another leaf. Make a few more of the leaves.

9. Attach the leaves around the crown.

10. Tie some ribbon in between the flowers or at the ends of the crown.

Easy Daisy Crown

Materials:

- Paper daisy flowers
- 1 piece 18" long thick wire
- 2 pieces 3" by 20" green crepe paper
- Green tape
- 1" by 6" ribbon, same as color as the dominant color of the flower
- Extra green paper
- Tissue paper
- 2" long thin wires

Directions:

1. Cut strips of tissue paper. Cover the thick wire with the tissue paper.

2. Bend the wire into a circle. Close it or leave a gap.

3. Cover the wire with green crepe paper or green tape.

4. Take the 2 pieces of 3" by 20" crepe paper. Fold them in half and cut fringes on the edges.

5. Open the strips and curl the fringes. Apply glue on the crease of one of the strips.

6. Place the green wire at the center of the strip. Make sure that there is a 1" allowance on each end if your crown is not a full circle. Cut the excess if your crown is a full circle.

7. Take the other strip. Apply glue at the center and cover the other side of the green wire.

8. Tie thin wires on your daisies. Leave at least 1" tail. Hide the wires with green tape.

9. Arrange the daisy flowers all over the crown.

10. Tie a bow at the back of the crown.

If your crown has a gap, thicken the tips with green tape. Cut your ribbons in half. Glue one part on each end of the crown. Use the ribbon to tie a bow.

Easy Baby's Breath Wreath or Crown

Materials:

- 4 pieces of 6" baby's breath flower as instructed in Chapter 6 (add more flowers if you desire)
- White ribbon, or any color that matches your flower
- Paper tape
- Other flowers, preferably peony and roses
- Thin wire
- Ribbons, optional

Directions:

1. Bend the baby's breath stalks and connect them until you've managed to create a circle. Connect the stalks by tying the ends with thin wire. Cover the wire with white or green paper tape.

2. Add bigger flowers on the vacant spaces or you can fill this in with more baby's breath flowers.

3. Add a design to the backside of the crown with more flowers, if desired.

Note: You can opt to exchange the baby's breath stalk with other cluster flowers such as the bells of Ireland.

Paper Flower Designed Jars

Materials:

- Crepe papers or Japanese paper
- Large sunflower, calendula or peony
- 2 half-bloom buds of the flower of choice
- leaves
- Thick and thin wires
- Tissue paper
- Green paper
- Mason jars
- Paper Name tag
- Hot glue

Directions:

1. Cut 6" by 24" strip of paper. Gather the paper from the top to bottom and twist them together until it form a twisted, flat paper rope.

2. Wrap the flat paper rope around the Mason jar. Cover the half-bottom of the jar.

3. Measure the circumference of the covered portion of the jar. Cut a flexible thick wire with the same measurement.

4. Thicken the wire with tissue and cover with two layers of green paper.

5. Wrap a thin wire at the bottom of the flower. Cover it with green paper or tape.

6. Tie the flower on the center of the small wreath. Add the half-bloomed buds beside it.

7. Attach the name tag next to any of the half-bloomed buds.

8. Add leaves around the wreath. Use the method taught in making the Rose Crown.

9. Attach the wreath on the jar. Secure with hot glue.

These next steps are optional:

10. Cover the lid of the jar with crepe or any wrapping paper.

11. Place a kirigami flower in the center of the lid.

2D - 3D Mural

You have a vacant wall, but you do not have enough money to buy a nice painting or a wallpaper to decorate it with? For that, you might want to try putting together a floral paper mural.

Materials:

- Drawings or printouts of any flowers, with long stems
- 3D flower that is similar and the same size as the flower you printed
- A drawing paper or canvass
- Water color or acrylic paints

Directions:
1. Draw a back drop on the drawing paper or canvass. You can draw a valley or a garden. If you're not too god with drawing, printing out a photo would work just as well.

2. Make the 3d flowers. Arrange them following the outline of your drawing or photo.

3. Cut the stems of the printed flowers and past them below the 3d Flowers.

4. Hang your drawing on the vacant wall.

Fake Terrariums

Flower terrariums can add elegance to a room, but real ones can sometimes be difficult to make and maintain. If you want something a little less demanding of your time and would last for a long while, fake terrariums with paper flowers would look just as great as the real thing!

Materials:

- A complete set of iris flower, narcissus, tulip or anthurium (one flower, one bud, and one or more leaves)
- 1 cylindrical vase with lid, make sure that it can fit the flower
- Handful of Shredded brown paper
- Handful of Shredded black paper
- Handful of dark red paper
- Handful of Shredded green paper
- Black paper
- Stones or marbles
- Strong cork

Directions:

1. Punch the flower in a cork block or a small Styrofoam ball.

2. Cover the cork or ball with black crepe paper or newspaper.

3. Insert the flower into the base.

4. Slowly place the marbles in the bottom of the vase until the ball is covered and the flower can stand on its own.

5. Combine the brown, red and black paper. Put them above the marbles. If some of the paper fall on the flower, carefully brush it with soft paint brush.

6. Top with green paper.

7. Add other elements like clean rocks or dried twigs.

8. Cover the terrarium and display.

Note: You can also use other shapes of aquarium, but the bases for the terrarium would still be the same.

You can also try making fake flower pot, using the same materials, but do not marbles at the bottom. Place some shells or real stones instead. You can also use real soil.

Conclusion

Thank you again for purchasing this book.

I understand that paper flower making can be challenging at times because of the steps and the details you have to make. Hence, I encourage you to enjoy the process and do not pressure yourself. Always think about how beautiful your project would look like because of the paper flowers and your efforts.

Lastly, do not limit your creativity with only the flowers included here. Some of the flowers have the same characteristics as some of the flowers discussed here. They only vary in sizes and color. You can apply the patterns and the methods in the book to create more flowers.

I hope you enjoyed the book. Keep safe, be healthy and bloom happily like the flowers you will make.

Manufactured by Amazon.ca
Bolton, ON